DEDICATED TO:
Trish, John Brian and Sarah Marie

By the same author, Brian Carthy:

Football Captains 1940–1993

The Championship 1995 – Football and Hurling
The Championship 1996 – Football and Hurling
The Championship 1997 – Football and Hurling
The Championship 1998 – Football and Hurling
The Championship 1999 – Football and Hurling
The Championship 2000 – Football and Hurling
The Championship 2001 – Football and Hurling
The Championship 2002 – Football and Hurling
The Championship 2003 – Football and Hurling
The Championship 2004 – Football and Hurling
The Championship 2005 – Football and Hurling
The Championship 2006 – Football and Hurling
The Championship 2007 – Football and Hurling
The Championship 2008 – Football and Hurling
The Championship 2009 – Football and Hurling
The Championship 2010 – Football and Hurling
The Championship 2011 – Football and Hurling
The Championship 2012 – Football and Hurling
The Championship 2013 – Football and Hurling
The Championship 2014 – Football and Hurling
The Championship 2015 – Football and Hurling
The Championship 2016 – Football and Hurling
The Championship 2017 – Football and Hurling
The Championship 2018 – Football and Hurling
The Championship 2019 – Football and Hurling

All-Ireland Football Finals 1995 - 2019

All Championship books listed above from 2000 onwards
plus *All-Ireland Football Finals 1995 - 2019* are available from:

SLIABH BÁN
PRODUCTIONS

Contact by email: sliabhbanproductions1@gmail.com
© Brian Carthy, 2020

**SLIABH BÁN
PRODUCTIONS**

Books available to order from:
sliabhbanproductions1@gmail.com

ISBN: 978-1-9993549-3-0

A CIP record of this book is available from the British Library.

Cover Design: Denise Campbell
Photography: Sportsfile
Layout and design: Denise Campbell
Printed in Ireland by PB Print Solution

Front cover: Stephen Cluxton, Dublin; Declan O'Sullivan, Kerry; Peter Canavan, Tyrone;
Jason Sherlock, Dublin; Maurice Fitzgerald, Kerry; Trevor Giles, Meath; Pádraic Joyce, Galway;
Donncha O'Connor, Cork; Michael Murphy, Donegal; Kieran McGeeney, Armagh

The author and publisher would like to thank all the people who assisted with the
publication of this book, especially Sliabh Bán Project managers,
John Brian Carthy and Sarah Marie Carthy.

Special thanks also to Denise Campbell, Louise Sharkey, Michael Dundon and
Ray McManus & his Sportsfile team for permission to use their photographs.

CONTENTS

All-Ireland Football Finals

Brian Carthy

Foreword

When the curtain came down on the 2019 Football Championship on Saturday, September 14 and mighty Dublin had become the first team ever to win five successive All-Ireland titles – a monumental sporting achievement - no one could have possibly foreseen what lay in store.

As it transpired, it would be well over 12 months later before another ball would be kicked in the inter-county football championship, as Covid 19 wreaked havoc on our nation and several other countries.

But in the midst of the heartbreaking loss of life and the deep sadness families suffered because of the coronavirus, there emerged vibrant and re-energised communities who rallied around those most in need.

All sporting organisations have been superb, including the GAA fraternity, who responded magnificently and with the utmost dignity to the many serious challenges their members faced because of the pandemic, most especially during lockdown.

Everyone was just happy and relieved when the club season got up and running, albeit with essential safety measures to curtail the spread of the virus.

And there was a palpable sense of excitement when the football and hurling inter-county championships were given the all-clear to go ahead in October.

I have been writing the annual record of the 'Football and Hurling Championships' since 1995, but because of the late, late start to this year's inter-county championships, clearly it was not possible to produce my yearly book before Christmas.

Therefore, because of the changed circumstances, I decided to write reports on the All-Ireland football finals from 1995, the first year I began compiling the Championship series up to 2019 when Dublin, under the management of Jim Gavin and the captaincy of Stephen Cluxton, marched into the history books.

There have been so many memorable football finals in Croke Park over the course of nearly a quarter-of-a-century which featured some of the most outstanding players ever to play the game.

No fewer than 8 counties have garnered All-Ireland football titles between 1995 and 2019 with Dublin leading the way during that golden period with victories in 1995, 2011, 2013 and the historic five-in-row from 2015 to 2019.

A grand total of 8 for the Dubs, six of those under the management of Gavin, who was a member of the team that claimed ultimate honours in 1995 when Pat Gilroy, the man in charge in 2011, came on as a substitute in the final, 16 years previously.

Dublin, captained by goalkeeper, John O'Leary, defeated Tyrone in that 1995 final by a single point on a 1-10 to 0-12 scoreline as the Sam Maguire Cup came to the capital city for the first time in 12 years.

24 years later, September 14, 2019, another Dublin goalkeeper, Stephen Cluxton led his county to a historic five successive titles with a replay victory over Kerry.

Incredibly, Parnells clubman, Cluxton, the most outstanding goalkeeper in living memory, raised the Sam Maguire Cup as Dublin captain on six occasions, 2013, 2015, 2016, 2017, 2018 and 2019.

Bryan Cullen was the captain on a memorable September Sunday in 2011 when the ice-cool Cluxton kicked a last-gasp free to steer Dublin through in what was one of the most drama-filled conclusions to a final in living memory.

It was also Dublin's first success on All-Ireland final day since 1995.

Incredibly, Brian Fenton, who has won five All-Ireland medals to date, has never lost a match in senior championship football; the same applies for more recent regular Dublin starters like Con O'Callaghan, Eoin Murchan, Niall Scully, David Byrne, John Small and Brian Howard.

Kerry claimed seven of the last 25 All-Irelands with victories in 1997, 2000 after a replay, 2004, 2006, 2007, 2009 and 2014.

Maurice Fitzgerald, one of the most outstanding and graceful footballers of his generation, scored 9 points as Kerry defeated Mayo in the 1997 final by 0-13 to 1-7 with the hugely-gifted Ciarán McDonald scoring the goal for the Connacht champions.

Kerry featured in 15 All-Ireland finals from 1997 to 2019 (including draws and replays in both 2000 and 2019) and recorded victories over Mayo in 1997, 2004 and 2006; Galway after a replay in 2000; Cork in 2007 and 2009 while the Kingdom overcame Donegal at the final hurdle in 2014.

However, Kerry suffered final day defeats against Armagh in 2002; Tyrone in 2005 and 2008 and Dublin in 2011, 2015 and 2019 after a replay.

Declan O'Sullivan was the Kerry captain in both 2006 and 2007.

Another double winning captain, Brian Dooher was central to Tyrone's three memorable All-Ireland final successes in 2003, 2005 and 2008 in what was a quite extraordinary decade for the county footballers under the management of the legendary Mickey Harte.

One of the all-time greats, Peter Canavan was the inspirational Tyrone captain in their maiden All-Ireland success in 2003 – some 8 years after registering 11 scores in the 1995 final, the same as Dublin's tally, yet the Errigal Ciaran clubman finished up on the losing side.

Meath, with the great Seán Boylan in charge, claimed ultimate honours in 1996 and 1999 while Mayo native, John O'Mahony, also proved his pedigree as an outstanding manager by guiding Galway to impressive Final day successes in 1998 against Kildare, after a 32-year gap and again in 2001 as the Tribesmen overcame Meath in the football showpiece.

The other All-Ireland winners between 1995 and 2019 were first-timers Armagh, who lit up the championship in 2002; resilient Cork in 2010 after a 20 year break and brave Donegal in 2012 – some two decades after their never-to-be-forgotten breakthrough in 1992.

Everyone will have their own special memories of September Sundays in Croke Park over the past quarter-of-a-century when the winners experienced unconfined joy and the vanquished had to endure heartbreaking loss.

No one suffered more on big-match days in Croke from 1995 to 2019 than proud Mayo who played in 10 All-Ireland finals during that period, including two replays in 1996 and 2016, but failed to land the ultimate prize, despite herculean efforts by some of the most outstanding players of this generation.

May 26, 2020 was the 40th anniversary of my arrival in RTÉ and, despite having never commentated on an All-Ireland senior final, I have had the privilege of covering memorable football, hurling, camogie and ladies football games from the mid-to-late 80's onwards.

When I wrote the 'Football Captains, All-Ireland Winners' book back in 1993, I did so to illustrate the significance of bringing home the Sam Maguire Cup and the excitement of unforgettable games and scores.

Nothing has changed.

Sport brings so much pleasure to everyone; the fun and the anecdotes, the emotions of defeat as well as triumph and the qualities – the vast disparate range of qualities – that make great individual players into great team players.

On a personal note, I want to thank all those in the Gaelic Games community, North, South, East, West and overseas, who have been so kind and helpful to me in my role as RTÉ Gaelic Games Correspondent/Commentator through the years as I covered games and did my best to break stories of interest to our listeners.

My sincerest thanks to the players, of course, at all levels, past and present, but also managers, officials and all those others in clubs and grounds, and towns and villages around the country who have made my work, not so much a career, as a recreation.

It has always been a deep privilege, an honour and a joy to travel the country and to be welcomed in the heartlands of our games, to enjoy the friendship and encouragement and co-operation of so many - great and good people - those loyal stalwarts upon whom the continued vibrancy of football, hurling, ladies football and camogie depends.

For decades now, commentating and reporting for RTÉ Radio, I have been blessed to be close to the GAA's unfolding dramas, not only on the field of play but also in committee rooms, and to convey the facts to the listener.

And whatever enjoyment it entailed, I have always been keenly aware of how privileged I am of the responsibility to be accurate and fair at all times.

I always felt it was vitally important to reflect accurately, not just the good, but also the unpleasantness that besets the GAA, from time to time.

I am already eagerly anticipating the years beyond.

I look forward to travelling the same roads and meeting many of the same people in an ever-changing landscape.

Of course the games themselves will continue to be full of colour and passion: new heroes will emerge, others will pass on the baton; teams will suddenly prosper - or unexpectedly regress; there will be important developments in the GAA and heated debates over many issues.

The future is exciting and challenging, not only for the GAA itself but also for the broadcast and print media dedicated to reporting on its activities.

I hope, God willing, to continue to make my own modest contribution for a few more years.

Grateful thanks to Trish, John Brian and Sarah Marie for their support at all times.

Brian Carthy
October 2020

ALL-IRELAND CHAMPIONS 1995 - 2019

1995
ALL–IRELAND
FOOTBALL FINAL

SUNDAY, SEPTEMBER 17

DUBLIN VERSUS TYRONE

CROKE PARK

REFEREE: PADDY RUSSELL
(TIPPERARY)

DUBLIN 1-10 TYRONE 0-12

There are certain images of All-Ireland Football Final Day 1995 that will linger in my mind long after other aspects of the game itself have become a distant memory.

I will never forget the concentration on Peter Canavan's face as he wrestled with the ball in the dying moments of the game after losing his footing.

Yet the brilliant full-forward was somehow able to deliver what appeared to be a legitimate pass to Seán McLoughlin, who sent the ball over the bar to level the game.

But referee Paddy Russell disallowed the score because, as he viewed it, Canavan handled the ball on the ground.

It was a controversial decision that generated much debate.

Canavan was the hero in the final and registered 11 scores, the same as the entire Dublin team, and yet ended up on the losing side.

Apart from Canavan, the only other Tyrone player to score was Jody Gormley.

Another image of the final is that of Dublin forward Charlie Redmond continuing to play on for a short time after being sent off.

And who could forget the smile on the face of proud Dublin manager, Dr. Pat O'Neill when he realised his team had claimed that much sought-after victory.

Dr. Pat was a relieved man that Dublin had at last won the title after a 12 year gap.

He was devastated after the 1994 All-Ireland final loss to Down, so all that mattered was that Dublin won the title in 1995.

Dublin had played some vintage football in preceding years and yet failed to win the ultimate prize, so the manner of victory was irrelevant in what was an uninspiring game.

Conditions at Croke Park were perfect for this most eagerly-awaited final.

Outsiders Tyrone, endeavouring to make it five-in-a-row for the province of Ulster, started at a blistering pace and unsettled Dublin.

Canavan kicked over two frees and then set up Gormley for Tyrone's third point.

The Dublin defence was under pressure early on but Paul Curran and Keith Barr responded to the Tyrone challenge with vigour.

In fact, Barr opened the scoring for Dublin with a long-range free and further points from Redmond and Paul Clarke levelled the match after ten minutes of play.

Dessie Farrell and Jason Sherlock began finding gaps in the Tyrone defence as Paul Bealin and Brian Stynes worked extremely hard in the midfield sector against the formidable Tyrone duo, Fergal Logan and Gormley, who never wilted in their pursuit of victory.

Farrell kicked three points before Redmond goaled for Dublin in the 26th minute after Sherlock slipped the ball through, despite a touch from Tyrone keeper Finbar McConnell, who was left completely exposed.

Jim Gavin then landed a point from play for Dublin just before the break.

The Dubs held a 1-8 to 0-6 advantage at half-time as Tyrone failed to deliver on their early promise.

Peter Canavan scored 5 points in the opening half.

Whereas Canavan rightly deserved the plaudits for his superb display throughout the game, credit must be given to every Tyrone player who gave their all in the course of a very physical encounter.

Dublin's work ethic was immense and this was best epitomised by Curran, Barr and Mick Deegan in the half-back line.

Canavan was quickly to the fore after the break when he kicked two frees and landed one from play.

Farrell calmed Dublin's nerves with a superb point.

The Dublin players' battled ferociously to limit the supply of ball to Canavan in the inside forward line.

If the scores were in short supply in the second half, there was more than a fair share of controversy.

Redmond, injured in the week leading up to the game, received his marching orders after 11 minutes of the second half but the drama was only beginning.

It was all very confusing.

Nearly three minutes after his dismissal, Redmond was still involved in the action.

The referee approached Redmond again and the brilliant Dublin forward eventually made the lonely walk to the line.

It was a bizarre episode.

Paul Clarke assumed the role of free-taker, but he was off target on a number of occasions.

Dublin failed to put away their chances and Tyrone weathered the storm.

Canavan kicked over a point but the hard-working Clarke made amends for earlier misses with a truly excellent point from play.

The Dublin defence was now under intense scrutiny; Canavan pointed two frees to reduce the deficit to the minimum and when Seán McLoughlin sent the ball over the bar in injury-time, everyone was certain there was going to be a replay.

Russell deemed otherwise and adjudged Canavan handled the ball on the ground.

He awarded a free out to Dublin, much to the frustration of Tyrone players and supporters.

The sound of the final whistle soon afterwards was sweet music to the ears of the Dublin players and management team.

Some of the Tyrone players were certain that the game had ended in a draw, unaware that McLoughlin's point had been disallowed.

Tyrone full-back, Chris Lawn told me after the game that he only realised Dublin had won when he saw their supporters streaming onto the field at the end.

He was devastated when the scoreboard revealed his worst fears and that Dublin had beaten Tyrone by a single point, 1-10 to 0-12.

And so the Sam Maguire Cup came back to the capital for the first time in 12 years, but for a courageous Ciarán Corr and his Tyrone team, it was a case of what might have been.

Dublin captain, John O'Leary

1995 ALL–IRELAND
SENIOR FOOTBALL CHAMPIONSHIP FINAL

SCORERS – DUBLIN: Dessie Farrell 0-4; Charlie Redmond 1-1; Paul Clarke 0-2;
Jim Gavin 0-1; Keith Barr 0-1; Paul Curran 0-1

SCORERS – TYRONE: Peter Canavan 0-11; Jody Gormley 0-1

DUBLIN

John O'Leary *(Captain)*

Paddy Moran	Ciarán Walsh	Keith Galvin
Paul Curran	Keith Barr	Mick Deegan

Paul Bealin   Brian Stynes

Jim Gavin	Dessie Farrell	Paul Clarke
Mick Galvin	Jason Sherlock	Charlie Redmond

SUBSTITUTES: Pat Gilroy for Keith Galvin; Robbie Boyle for Mick Galvin;
Vinnie Murphy for Dessie Farrell

TYRONE

Finbar McConnell

Paul Devlin	Chris Lawn	Fay Devlin
Ronan McGarrity	Séamus McCallan	Seán McLoughlin

Fergal Logan   Jody Gormley

Ciarán Corr *(Captain)*	Pascal Canavan	Ciarán Loughran
Ciarán McBride	Peter Canavan	Stephen Lawn

SUBSTITUTES: Mattie McGleenan for Ciarán Loughran;
Brian Gormley for Stephen Lawn;
Paul Donnelly for Séamus McCallan

DUBLIN - 1995

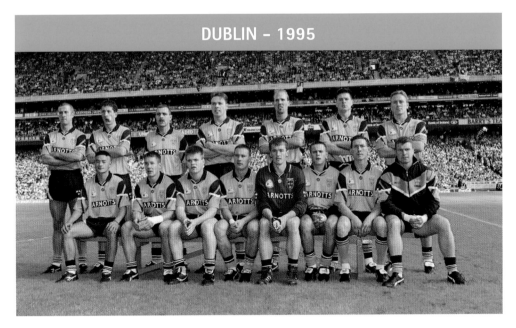

Back Row, left to right: Paul Clarke, Mick Galvin, Ciarán Walsh,
Paul Bealin, Brian Stynes, Paddy Moran, Keith Barr
Front Row, left to right: Jason Sherlock, Jim Gavin, Dessie Farrell,
Paul Curran, John O'Leary, Keith Galvin, Mick Deegan, Charlie Redmond

Dublin manager, Dr. Pat O'Neill

1995 ALL-STARS FOOTBALL SELECTION

John O'Leary
(Dublin) 5th

Tony Scullion
(Derry) 4th

Mark O'Connor
(Cork) 1st

Fay Devlin
(Tyrone) 1st

Paul Curran
(Dublin) 2nd

Keith Barr
(Dublin) 2nd

Steven O'Brien
(Cork) 3rd

Brian Stynes
(Dublin) 1st

Anthony Tohill
(Derry) 3rd

Ja Fallon
(Galway) 1st

Dessie Farrell
(Dublin) 1st

Paul Clarke
(Dublin) 1st

Tommy Dowd
(Meath) 3rd

Peter Canavan
(Tyrone) 2nd

Charlie Redmond
(Dublin) 3rd

1996
ALL-IRELAND
FOOTBALL FINAL
REPLAY

SUNDAY, SEPTEMBER 29

MEATH VERSUS MAYO

CROKE PARK

REFEREE: PAT McENANEY
(MONAGHAN)

MEATH 2-9 MAYO 1-11

The 1996 All-Ireland football final replay between Meath and Mayo will be remembered as the day of the big fight and the big wind.

The game was underway little more than five minutes when a brawl broke out involving several players from both sides.

Once the first punches were thrown, players arrived from all directions to flex their muscles and make their unwanted contributions.

Referee Pat McEnaney was faced with an extremely difficult decision as there were numerous players involved in the fracas.

So, after consultation with his officials, McEnaney singled out Mayo midfielder Liam McHale and Meath half-back Colm Coyle, for the ultimate punishment.

It was the worst possible scenario for Mayo.

McHale was their key player and was Man-of-the Match in the drawn game.

Coyle had emerged as the Meath hero when he scored the dramatic equalising point as his long-range effort bounced over the bar to force a replay for the first time since 1988.

The replay was a game Mayo should have won, but Meath deserve every credit for their magnificent fightback against the odds.

Mayo had the advantage of the strong wind during the opening half, but, despite an abundance of possession, only led at the interval by four points after Trevor Giles scored a penalty for Meath just before half-time.

Mayo played their best football when facing the wind in the second half, but similar to the drawn game, paid the ultimate price for their inability to convert scoring opportunities and make good their superiority in many areas of the field.

Meath had reduced the margin to a single point within five minutes of the re-start.

But, against the odds, the Connacht champions, still held on to the lead until inspirational Meath captain, Tommy Dowd scored a goal ten minutes from time to edge his side one point ahead.

James Horan levelled the game in the closing minutes before Brendan Reilly landed the winning point to ensure his name will forever be indelibly linked with the 1996 All-Ireland final replay.

Meath were never allowed to control the game, but through resilience and self-belief, Seán Boylan's brave team fashioned a famous victory.

Dowd played a captain's role contributing 1-3 of his team's total as well as winning the penalty, converted by Giles, who also had an immense influence and scored 1-4.

Martin O'Connell was an influential player at all times, but was particularly effective in the first half when his steadying influence and well-directed clearances proved vital for Meath.

James Horan turned in an outstanding display for Mayo and kicked five points from play while his teammate, Maurice Sheridan, once again underlined his worth with five points, including a superb effort from play in the second half.

One of the highlights of the first half was a truly splendid goal from Mayo substitute, P.J. Loftus, who had replaced Ray Dempsey after just 26 minutes.

Loftus latched on to a breaking ball and raced through the Meath defence to send a powerful shot past goalkeeper, Conor Martin.

But Meath hit back with a goal from a penalty by Giles.

Sheridan scored a point from a free in injury-time to move his side four points ahead at the interval, 1-6 to 1-2 - a lead which hardly reflected Mayo's first half superiority.

Meath scored three points from play, two from Dowd and one from Giles, within five minutes of the re-start, which cut the deficit to a single point.

With a strong breeze behind them, it seemed only a matter of time until Meath would take control and run out comfortable winners.

Mayo never allowed that to happen and played some outstanding football in the second half, bravely defying the odds.

The Mayo defence stood firm while further-afield, David Brady, substitute Pat Fallon, Colm McManamon, Horan and Sheridan all battled bravely against the elements but Meath, inspired by O'Connell, Dowd and Giles simply refused to yield.

Both teams displayed passion, commitment and courage in a 'do or die' effort' to win the game.

The odds favoured Mayo when Horan landed a point to edge his side two clear but Dowd, despite being fouled, somehow managed to score a crucial goal to put Meath ahead for the very first time.

Mayo forward John Casey had his pass intercepted by Enda McManus whose long clearance found Graham Geraghty, who was fouled by Pat Holmes.

Geraghty took a quick free to Dowd, who scored the crucial goal to put Meath in front for the very first time.

Horan then levelled the match before Reilly sent over the winning point.

Meath captain, Tommy Dowd

SCORERS – MEATH: Trevor Giles 1-4; Tommy Dowd 1-3; Barry Callaghan 0-1; Brendan Reilly 0-1

SCORERS – MAYO: James Horan 0-5; Maurice Sheridan 0-5; P.J. Loftus 1-0; John Casey 0-1

MEATH

Conor Martin

Mark O'Reilly   Darren Fay   Martin O'Connell

Colm Coyle   Enda McManus   Paddy Reynolds

Jimmy McGuinness   John McDermott

Trevor Giles   Tommy Dowd *(Captain)*   Graham Geraghty

Colm Brady   Brendan Reilly   Barry Callaghan

SUBSTITUTES: Jody Devine for Barry Callaghan; Ollie Murphy for Brendan Reilly

MAYO

John Madden

Kenneth Mortimer   Kevin Cahill   Dermot Flanagan

Pat Holmes   James Nallen   Noel Connelly *(Captain)*

Liam McHale   David Brady

James Horan   Colm McManamon   Maurice Sheridan

Anthony Finnerty   John Casey   Ray Dempsey

SUBSTITUTES: P.J. Loftus for Ray Dempsey; Pat Fallon for Dermot Flanagan; Tom Reilly for Anthony Finnerty

MEATH – 1996 (REPLAY)

Back row, left to right: Trevor Giles, Graham Geraghty, John McDermott, Jimmy McGuinness,
Barry Callaghan, Martin O'Connell, Colm Brady, Tommy Dowd, Brendan Reilly
Front row, left to right: Paddy Reynolds, Mark O'Reilly, Colm Coyle,
Conor Martin, Darren Fay, Enda McManus

Meath manager, Seán Boylan

1996 ALL-STARS FOOTBALL SELECTION

Finbar McConnell
(Tyrone) 1st

Kenneth Mortimer
(Mayo) 1st

Darren Fay
(Meath) 1st

Martin O'Connell
(Meath) 4th

Pat Holmes
(Mayo) 1st

James Nallen
(Mayo) 1st

Paul Curran
(Dublin) 3rd

Liam McHale
(Mayo) 1st

John McDermott
(Meath) 1st

Trevor Giles
(Meath) 1st

Tommy Dowd
(Meath) 4th

James Horan
(Mayo) 1st

Joe Brolly
(Derry) 1st

Peter Canavan
(Tyrone) 3rd

Maurice Fitzgerald
(Kerry) 2nd

1997
ALL-IRELAND
FOOTBALL FINAL

SUNDAY, SEPTEMBER 28

KERRY VERSUS MAYO

CROKE PARK

REFEREE: BRIAN WHITE
(WEXFORD)

KERRY 0-13 MAYO 1-7

1997 was the year when Kerry football, once again, took its place at the top table and Maurice Fitzgerald, one of the finest footballers of his generation, finally got his hands on that elusive All-Ireland medal.

Fitzgerald exuded class and turned in a superlative display on a day when Kerry claimed their 31st All-Ireland title with a three points victory over Mayo.

The St. Mary's, Cahirciveen clubman scored nine points and decorated the greatest sporting day of the year with a vast array of skills to underline his class.

Fitzgerald's performance was all the more significant given the fact that he was involved in an accidental collision with his team-mate, Billy O'Shea, after just 16 minutes.

O'Shea was forced to retire with a compound fracture of the ankle.

Play was held up for nearly five minutes before the Laune Rangers player was transferred to the Mater Hospital in Dublin.

It was cruel luck on O'Shea, an exceptionally talented player, who had been very prominent before his unfortunate injury.

By that stage, Fitzgerald had scored a point from a free but otherwise had hardly touched the ball.

One wondered what thoughts were running through his mind when he saw his colleague being stretchered off the field.

It was clear Fitzgerald was upset to see O'Shea in such pain.

It was a real test of Fitzgerald's character and he rose to the challenge majestically.

Johnny Crowley was called into the fray in place of the injured O'Shea.

Pa Laide and Darragh Ó Sé had scored the opening two points of the game as Kerry took control from the early stages.

Mayo suffered a setback as early as the fourth minute when the vastly experienced Dermot Flanagan, a real leader, had to retire injured to be replaced by James Horan, as manager John Maughan was forced to reshuffle his team.

But already a pattern was developing.

Centre-half-back, Liam O'Flaherty and midfielder, Darragh O'Sé were establishing superiority early on, while Pa Laide was adding to his reputation with a fine display.

William Kirby worked tirelessly to complement Ó Sé while, all around the field, Kerry won many of the personal duels as Mayo missed several chances from eminently scorable positions.

Ciarán McDonald was surprised to see one umpire signal a point and the other wave wide after 15 minutes as Mayo struggled to make an impact.

In fact, 23 minutes had elapsed before the Connacht champions opened their account through a long-range free from Maurice Sheridan.

Fitzgerald struck over a superb point from play after 25 minutes as Kerry tightened their grip on the game.

Sheridan closed the gap with a pointed free, but Laide responded for Kerry with a fisted point.

Fitzgerald and Sheridan exchanged points to leave Kerry 0-7 to 0-3 ahead after 36 minutes.

However, it was noticeable that Sheridan was limping badly when he scored his third point and the Balla marksman was unable to re-appear for the second half because of a hamstring injury.

Liam McHale was moved to midfield late in the first half, but Kerry finished the stronger with Fitzgerald kicking his fifth point to give the Munster champions an 0-8 to 0-3 interval lead.

Colm McManamon missed a gilt-edged chance of a score just before the half-time whistle when he shot wide from in front of the posts.

Sheridan was replaced by Diarmuid Byrne at the start of the second half as Mayo set about the onerous task of turning the tide.

McDonald pointed from a close-in free while Mayo goalkeeper Peter Burke brought off a fine save, but there was little respite as Kerry continued to apply the pressure.

Fitzgerald kicked two further points in quick succession; Burke denied Johnny Crowley a goal with another splendid save, but inside a minute the Glenflesk clubman kicked a point from play to extend Kerry's lead to seven points.

By now the game had entered its most critical phase.

Kenneth Mortimer, Noel Connelly, Pat Fallon, McManamon, McHale and Horan inspired the Mayo comeback as Kerry came under intense pressure.

McManamon scored a fine point from play and then came the goal that Mayo so badly needed.

Barry O'Shea was penalised for fouling substitute Diarmuid Byrne and referee Brian White awarded a penalty which was superbly converted by McDonald to change the course of the game.

Now it was the turn of Kerry to experience the white heat of Final Day in Croke Park.

Horan, outstanding in the 1996 Final, transformed the game when he kicked over two magnificent scores from play to reduce the deficit to a single point.

Kerry appeared vulnerable.

Fitzgerald and Liam Hassett shot wide as Mayo sensed victory.

But when the need was greatest, Fitzgerald once again delivered and his 8th point edged Kerry 0-12 to 1-7 ahead.

The brilliant Peter Burke denied the hard-working Denis Dwyer a certain goal while at the other end of the field Mayo spurned chance after chance.

McDonald and P.J. Loftus were both off target from close range.

There is no doubt that Mayo had sufficient chances to win the game in the closing 20 minutes but poor marksmanship put paid to their All-Ireland final ambitions.

Kerry fought tenaciously in the closing tension-filled minutes to stave off resurgent Mayo and Fitzgerald scored a superb point with virtually the last kick of the game to ensure the Kingdom their first All-Ireland title in 11 years.

Kerry captain, Liam Hassett

1997 ALL–IRELAND
SENIOR FOOTBALL CHAMPIONSHIP FINAL

SCORERS – KERRY: Maurice Fitzgerald 0-9; Pa Laide 0-2; Darragh Ó Sé 0-1; Johnny Crowley 0-1

SCORERS – MAYO: Ciarán McDonald 1-1; Maurice Sheridan 0-3; James Horan 0-2; Colm McManamon 0-1

KERRY

Declan O'Keeffe

Killian Burns   Barry O'Shea   Stephen Stack

Séamus Moynihan   Liam O'Flaherty   Eamonn Breen

Darragh Ó Sé   William Kirby

Pa Laide   Liam Hassett *(Captain)*   Denis Dwyer

Billy O'Shea   Dara Ó Cinnéide   Maurice Fitzgerald

SUBSTITUTES: Johnny Crowley for Billy O'Shea; Donal Daly for William Kirby; Mike Frank Russell for Dara Ó Cinnéide

MAYO

Peter Burke

Pat Holmes   Kenneth Mortimer   Dermot Flanagan

Fergal Costello   James Nallen   Noel Connelly *(Captain)*

Pat Fallon   David Heaney

Maurice Sheridan   Colm McManamon   John Casey

Ciarán McDonald   Liam McHale   David Nestor

SUBSTITUTES: James Horan for Dermot Flanagan; Diarmuid Byrne for Maurice Sheridan; P.J. Loftus for David Nestor

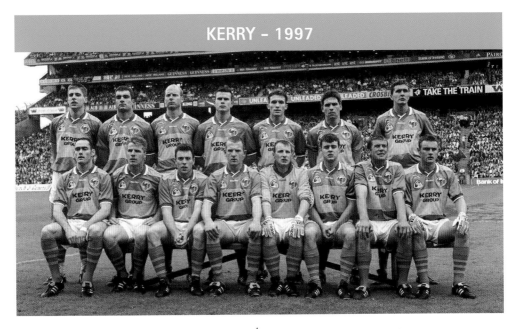

KERRY – 1997

Back Row, left to right: Darragh Ó Sé, Barry O'Shea, Liam O'Flaherty,
Killian Burns, Billy O'Shea, Stephen Stack, Maurice Fitzgerald
Front Row, left to right: Pa Laide, Eamonn Breen, Séamus Moynihan, Liam Hassett,
Declan O'Keeffe, Denis Dwyer, Dara Ó Cinnéide, William Kirby

Kerry manager, Páidí Ó Sé

1997 ALL-STARS FOOTBALL SELECTION

Declan O'Keeffe
(Kerry) 1st

Kenneth Mortimer
(Mayo) 2nd

Davy Dalton
(Kildare) 1st

Cathal Daly
(Offaly) 1st

Séamus Moynihan
(Kerry) 1st

Glen Ryan
(Kildare) 1st

Eamonn Breen
(Kerry) 1st

Pat Fallon
(Mayo) 1st

Niall Buckley
(Kildare) 1st

Pa Laide
(Kerry) 1st

Trevor Giles
(Meath) 2nd

Dermot McCabe
(Cavan) 1st

Joe Brolly
(Derry) 2nd

Brendan Reilly
(Meath) 1st

Maurice Fitzgerald
(Kerry) 3rd

1998 ALL–IRELAND FOOTBALL FINAL

SUNDAY, SEPTEMBER 27

GALWAY VERSUS KILDARE

CROKE PARK

REFEREE: JOHN BANNON
(LONGFORD)

GALWAY 1–14 KILDARE 1–10

Galway's thirty-two year wait ended on what proved to be a momentous day in Croke Park for Captain Ray Silke and his magnificent team in maroon and white.

Galway produced a storming second half display to overcome brave Kildare and claim the Sam Maguire Cup for the first time since 1966 when the legendary Enda Colleran captained the three-in-a-row team.

The game itself will be remembered, above all else, for the quality of football served up by Galway in the second half and the splendid individual displays of Michael Donnellan, Ja Fallon, Tomás Mannion, Seán Óg de Paor, John Divilly, Pádraic Joyce and midfielders, Kevin Walsh and Seán Ó Dómhnaill.

But every Galway player was a hero on a never-to-be-forgotten day for all involved with the team and their large following while Kildare, to their credit, never wilted in their pursuit of victory.

The contrasting styles of the two teams were very evident from early on in the contest.

Galway played much more direct football while Kildare, apart from a spell in the opening half, concentrated largely on the short-passing game.

Galway reaped rich dividends by relying on a more traditional style game, which worked to great effect, particularly in the second half when John O'Mahony's finely-tuned team proved the undoubted masters.

Galway outscored Kildare by 1-9 to 0-5 in the second half with the most stylish and positive football of the entire Championship.

It was always felt that Galway had the best forwards in the game and the players concerned certainly showcased their talents on the biggest day of the year.

The Galway defence overcame some shaky moments in the first half to make life extremely uncomfortable for the Kildare forwards while John Divilly produced an impressive display.

Walsh and Ó Domhnaill were a strong force at midfield for Galway although tested at times by Niall Buckley and Willie McCreery, who worked tirelessly throughout for Kildare.

Lightning-fast, Michael Donnellan turned in an inspirational display and his direct running, combined with his superb ball control, caused endless problems in the Kildare defence.

Donnellan won an abundance of possession all over the field and, most importantly, distributed it to telling effect time and again.

Tomás Mannion was outstanding at corner-back from start to finish and curbed the threat of the highly-skilful Kildare forward Martin Lynch.

Ja Fallon recovered from a quiet first half to produce an outstanding display after the break as Galway lifted the pace appreciably.

Fallon scored three points, including one from a superb sideline kick on the Hogan Stand side.

Kildare captain, Glen Ryan, despite a heavily strapped leg, was highly-effective at centre-half-back in the opening half but struggled after the break against a rejuvenated Fallon.

Goalkeeper Martin McNamara played a vital role in Galway's victory and varied his kick-outs with great accuracy to give his team a distinct advantage.

Galway started at a brisk pace with points from Joyce, Seán Óg de Paor and an excellent effort from Donnellan before Eddie McCormack opened Kildare's account with a point from play in the 14th minute.

Even at that early stage, Mannion was a huge influence in defence and continued this high-quality display throughout the entire match.

The game changed dramatically midway through the opening half when Dermot Earley palmed the ball to the Galway net following a pass from the hard-working McCreery.

Kildare's play improved immeasurably after Earley's goal while Galway, for a time, lost their way and their rhythm as the Leinster champions grew in confidence.

Kildare began to play a more direct brand of football and enjoyed their most fruitful period of the game but their dominance was not reflected on the scoreboard, mainly due to some quality defending by the Galway backs.

Declan Kerrigan kicked a fine point from play in the 23rd minute but Donnellan reduced the margin to the minimum with his second point from play after 29 minutes.

Galway struggled in the second quarter but Kildare were somehow unable to capitalise on all their hard-won possession.

Karl O'Dwyer scored two points from play late in the half for Kildare but Pádraig Gravin was unfortunate to slip with a goal on offer.

McCormack increased Kildare's lead in the 35th minute before Joyce closed the first half scoring with a pointed free in injury-time.

Still Kildare held a 1-5 to 0-5 advantage at the break.

There was a complete transformation of Galway's play for long stages in the second half and Kildare had few answers as the Connacht champions found new life and produced a magnificent display.

Fallon was in razor-sharp form after the break and he kicked over a splendid point within three minutes of the re-start.

Little more than a minute later, Joyce was celebrating after scoring the goal that turned the game decisively in Galway's favour.

Donnellan gathered Divilly's long clearance out of defence, and his pass set up Joyce, who evaded Kildare goalkeeper, Christy Byrne, before kicking the ball into the empty net.

Niall Finnegan and Fallon then landed a point each as Galway moved 1-8 to 1-5 ahead by the 43rd minute.

Galway were now in full stride and the impressive Finnegan scored his second point before substitute, Pádraig Brennan sent over Kildare's first point of the second half from a free.

With Galway largely on top in defence and midfield, their forwards were given an opportunity to showcase their undoubted talents.

Fallon scored a wonder point from a sideline kick in the 52nd minute to push Galway five points ahead - it was an inspirational score.

Brennan replied with a pointed free as Kildare battled bravely to force their way back into the game.

Ó Dómhnaill landed a blockbuster of a point from play while the ever-alert Kildare goalkeeper, Christy Byrne denied the energetic Derek Savage a goal with a fine save.

Finnegan then converted a free to leave Galway 1-13 to 1-7 ahead by the 57th minute.

Kildare's second half total up to that juncture was a meagre two points from frees by Brennan.

Brian Murphy made an impact when introduced from the bench in place of Martin Lynch.

Brennan, Buckley and Earley found the target to reduce the margin to just three points.

Earley's powerful shot was deflected over the crossbar by Galway corner-back, Tomás Meehan.

On such incidents, All-Ireland Finals are won and lost as Seán Óg de Paor sealed victory for Galway with a splendid point from play.

Murphy, though, hit the Galway post in injury-time to compound a frustrating day for a brave Kildare side that battled to the very end.

Galway captain, Ray Silke

SCORERS – GALWAY: Pádraic Joyce 1-2; Niall Finnegan 0-4; Ja Fallon 0-3; Michael Donnellan 0-2; Seán Óg de Paor 0-2; Seán Ó Dómhnaill 0-1

SCORERS – KILDARE: Dermot Earley 1-1; Pádraig Brennan 0-3; Eddie McCormack 0-2; Karl O'Dwyer 0-2; Niall Buckley 0-1; Declan Kerrigan 0-1

GALWAY

Martin McNamara

Tomás Meehan	Gary Fahey	Tomás Mannion
Ray Silke *(Captain)*	John Divilly	Seán Óg de Paor

Kevin Walsh   Seán Ó Dómhnaill

Shay Walsh	Ja Fallon	Michael Donnellan
Derek Savage	Pádraic Joyce	Niall Finnegan

SUBSTITUTE: Paul Clancy for Shay Walsh

KILDARE

Christy Byrne

Brian Lacey	John Finn	Ken Doyle
Sos Dowling	Glen Ryan *(Captain)*	Anthony Rainbow

Niall Buckley   Willie McCreery

Eddie McCormack	Declan Kerrigan	Dermot Earley
Martin Lynch	Karl O'Dwyer	Pádraig Gravin

SUBSTITUTES: Pádraig Brennan for Pádraig Gravin; Brian Murphy for Martin Lynch

GALWAY – 1998

Back row, left to right: Pádraic Joyce, Tomás Meehan, Shay Walsh, Ja Fallon,
Kevin Walsh, Seán Ó Dómhnaill, Gary Fahey, John Divilly
Front row, left ro right: Seán Óg de Paor, Michael Donnellan, Ray Silke, Derek Savage,
Martin McNamara, Niall Finnegan, Tomás Mannion

Galway manager, John O'Mahony

1998 ALL-STARS FOOTBALL SELECTION

Martin McNamara
(Galway) 1st

Brian Lacey
(Kildare) 1st

Seán Marty Lockhart
(Derry) 1st

Tomás Mannion
(Galway) 1st

John Finn
(Kildare) 1st

Glen Ryan
(Kildare) 2nd

Seán Óg de Paor
(Galway) 1st

John McDermott
(Meath) 2nd

Kevin Walsh
(Galway) 1st

Michael Donnellan
(Galway) 1st

Ja Fallon
(Galway) 2nd

Dermot Earley
(Kildare) 1st

Karl O'Dwyer
(Kildare) 1st

Pádraic Joyce
(Galway) 1st

Declan Browne
(Tipperary) 1st

1999 ALL-IRELAND FOOTBALL FINAL

SUNDAY, SEPTEMBER 26

MEATH VERSUS CORK

CROKE PARK

REFEREE: MICHAEL CURLEY (GALWAY)

MEATH 1-11 CORK 1-8

It was a day of unbridled joy for Meath footballers and their inspirational manager, Seán Boylan as the Royal County claimed their seventh All-Ireland title and the last of the Millennium, exactly fifty years after Brian Smyth captained the county to win their first crown in 1949.

Boylan, a wonderful ambassador for his county, was at the helm for four of those All-Ireland victories in 1987, 1988, 1996 and again in 1999 – a proud record which serves to underline his pedigree as one of the truly outstanding managers in the history of the game.

Mighty captain, Graham Geraghty was one happy man as he stood on the podium in the centre of Croke Park and addressed the Meath faithful all around the famous ground, before eventually raising the Sam Maguire Cup.

It was a memorable victory for a fiercely-committed Meath side against a strong-willed and tenacious Cork team, managed by the legendary, Larry Tompkins.

Cork had high hopes of adding the football title to the hurling crown, won two weeks earlier, but it was not to be, as Meath proved the masters and Fijian-born Seán Óg Ó hAilpín was deprived of the honour of joining Teddy McCarthy in the history books.

McCarthy still remains the only player to win All-Ireland hurling and football medals in the one year on the field of play.

Tommy Dowd, ruled out of the starting line-up because of injury, made a very brief appearance near the end of the game to complete a perfect day for Meath people everywhere.

This was a keenly-contested, physical encounter that was played in wet conditions, which proved extremely difficult.

As the game entered the final stage, Meath had the players that responded to the challenge with the ferocious determination, which has become the hallmark of Boylan's teams down through the years.

Meath held a three-point advantage at the break, but Cork were handed a lifeline early in the second half when goalkeeper, Kevin O'Dwyer saved a penalty from Trevor

Giles and, soon afterwards, Joe Kavanagh scored a magnificent goal for the Munster champions.

But Meath, displaying their renowned steely resolve, regained their composure and played some superb direct football to fashion a well-merited victory.

Trevor Giles, although off target from a number of frees, was a major influence and played a big role in Meath's victory, particularly in the closing quarter.

Mark O'Reilly was outstanding at corner-back; Enda McManus and Darren Fay were also impressive at various stages throughout the game; Evan Kelly and Geraghty scored three points each from play while Ollie Murphy took his goal splendidly.

Meath started at a brisk pace with a point each from Kelly and Giles before Mark O'Sullivan opened Cork's account with a point from play in the 10th minute.

Kavanagh and Donal Curtis exchanged points but Meath received a tremendous boost in the 25th minute when Murphy drove the ball past O'Dwyer for a superb goal.

Both sides continued to miss chances, but still there were good scores before half-time, none better than from the impressive Kelly, who landed two fine points to bring his first half tally to three.

Meath took a 1-5 to 0-5 lead into the break and had a glorious opportunity of increasing that lead shortly after the re-start when awarded a penalty after Geraghty was fouled.

Giles' shot was saved by O'Dwyer and it lifted Cork's spirits no end.

Philip Clifford, highly effective in the Cork attack, then landed a point and when Kavanagh blasted the ball to the Meath net for a stunning goal, the Munster champions had moved ahead for the very first time.

It was, perhaps, the one stage of the game that Cork looked likely to win, but it was not to be against a formidable Meath side, that never once relented in their pursuit of victory.

Cork persisted with short passing and it helped Meath force their way back into the game.

Notably, Meath raised the intensity after Kavanagh's goal which illustrated the immense quality of the Leinster champions when under pressure.

The Cork forward division struggled in the second half against a strong-running and tight-marking Meath defence that delivered early ball to their midfield and forward line with telling effect.

As the pressure mounted, Giles calmly converted a '45, which edged his side 1-9 to 1-8 ahead with little more than 10 minutes left to play.

Giles and Geraghty then tacked on a point each in the closing minutes to seal a famous victory on a memorable day for Meath football.

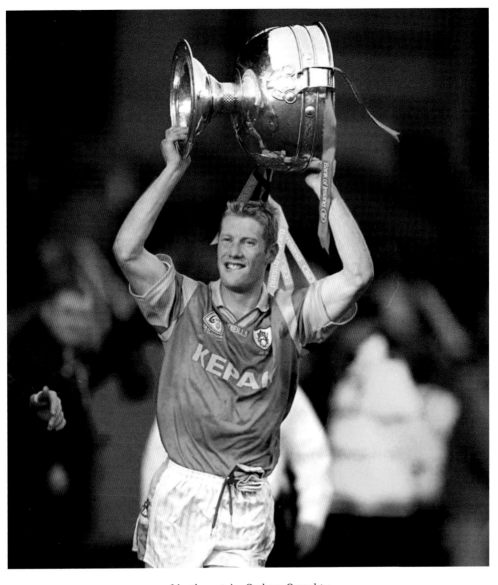

Meath captain, Graham Geraghty

SCORERS – MEATH: Trevor Giles 0-4; Graham Geraghty 0-3; Evan Kelly 0-3; Ollie Murphy 1-0; Donal Curtis 0-1

SCORERS – CORK: Philip Clifford 0-5; Joe Kavanagh 1-1; Podsie O'Mahony 0-1; Mark O'Sullivan 0-1

MEATH

Cormac Sullivan

Mark O'Reilly   Darren Fay   Cormac Murphy

Paddy Reynolds   Enda McManus   Hank Traynor

Nigel Crawford   John McDermott

Evan Kelly   Trevor Giles   Nigel Nestor

Ollie Murphy   Graham Geraghty *(Captain)*   Donal Curtis

SUBSTITUTES: Richie Kealy for Nigel Nestor; Barry Callaghan for Hank Traynor; Tommy Dowd for Evan Kelly

CORK

Kevin O'Dwyer

Ronan McCarthy   Seán Óg Ó hAilpín   Anthony Lynch

Ciarán O'Sullivan   Owen Sexton   Martin Cronin

Nicholas Murphy   Micheál O'Sullivan

Micheál Ó Cróinín   Joe Kavanagh   Podsie O'Mahony

Philip Clifford *(Captain)*   Don Davis   Mark O'Sullivan

SUBSTITUTES: Fionán Murray for Micheál O'Sullivan; Fachtna Collins for Micheál Ó Cróinín; Michael O'Donovan for Podsie O'Mahony

Back row, left to right: Trevor Giles, John McDermott, Graham Geraghty, Darren Fay,
Cormac Sullivan, Nigel Crawford, Hank Traynor, Nigel Nestor, Cormac Murphy
Front row, left to right: Mark O'Reilly, Donal Curtis, Evan Kelly,
Paddy Reynolds, Ollie Murphy, Enda McManus

Meath manager, Seán Boylan

1999 ALL-STARS FOOTBALL SELECTION

Kevin O'Dwyer
(Cork) 1st

Mark O'Reilly
(Meath) 1st

Darren Fay
(Meath) 2nd

Anthony Lynch
(Cork) 1st

Ciarán O'Sullivan
(Cork) 1st

Kieran McGeeney
(Armagh) 1st

Paddy Reynolds
(Meath) 1st

John McDermott
(Meath) 3rd

Ciarán Whelan
(Dublin) 1st

Diarmaid Marsden
(Armagh) 1st

Trevor Giles
(Meath) 3rd

James Horan
(Mayo) 2nd

Philip Clifford
(Cork) 1st

Graham Geraghty
(Meath) 2nd

Ollie Murphy
(Meath) 1st

2000
ALL–IRELAND
FOOTBALL FINAL
REPLAY

SATURDAY, OCTOBER 7

KERRY VERSUS GALWAY

CROKE PARK

REFEREE: BRIAN WHITE
(WEXFORD)

KERRY 0–17 GALWAY 1–10

It was a day of high emotion in Croke Park as Kerry deservedly claimed their 32nd All-Ireland title in a game that produced much quality football and which was embellished by more than a few outstanding individual displays.

Kerry captain Séamus Moynihan, a truly exceptional player, delivered a tour-de-force performance at full-back as he led his team to a famous victory.

Maurice Fitzgerald's class, once again, shone through when introduced from the subs bench.

It was Fitzgerald's sixth championship game in a row to be named among the substitutes, even though the '1997 Footballer of the Year' had made it abundantly clear before the final that he was in the shape of his life.

Fitzgerald delivered a fine display, particularly in the closing 25 minutes after he moved outfield.

What was most noticeable was the understanding between Fitzgerald and Mike Frank Russell, who thrived on the quality of ball from the St. Mary's man.

Russell spoke to me live on RTÉ Radio One immediately after the game and heaped praise on Fitzgerald, calling him the 'Mick O'Connell of his era'.

The Galway full-forward line of Derek Savage, Pádraic Joyce and Niall Finnegan struggled to make a real impact against the very impressive Mike McCarthy; 'Man of the Match', Moynihan and Mike Hassett.

Mike's brother, Liam, the 1997 All-Ireland winning captain, made a very significant input to the victory, scoring three points from play, the same total as impressive corner-forward, Johnny Crowley.

The Kerry half-backs and midfield also played their part and the forward division caused some serious problems for a hard-pressed Galway defence.

It was easily Kerry's most balanced and consistent performance of the entire championship, as the players kept their composure throughout in what was the first All-Ireland final to be played on a Saturday.

Crowley had the Kerry flags flying within seconds of the start when he kicked over a fine point, but Galway were soon on the move with a stunning goal scored by Declan Meehan in the 6th minute.

Kevin Walsh gathered the ball in his own goalmouth and began a move upfield, which involved no fewer than seven passes.

Paul Clancy eventually kicked the ball into the path of the energetic Meehan, who crashed the ball to the corner of the Kerry net.

It was a wonder goal, pure and simple, and it will forever remain as one of the major highlights of the 2000 final and a fitting testament to an outstanding Galway team that gave their all in search of victory.

Galway missed the influence of Ja Fallon, ruled out with injury, most especially after Walsh had to retire after just 16 minutes of play.

Walsh entered the fray again in the second half, and even though he was still clearly hampered by injury, the giant midfielder scored a point from play, as he tried with all his might to turn the tide.

Dara Ó Cinnéide levelled the match for the first time with a pointed free in the 17th minute, but Michael Donnellan replied with a point for Galway.

Eamonn Fitzmaurice, Noel Kennelly and Liam Hassett rowed in with a point each as an improving Kerry team began to dictate the pace.

Joe Bergin, who replaced the injured Walsh, landed a point from play while Ó Cinnéide completed the first half scoring with a third pointed free to leave Kerry, 0-8 to 1-3, in front at half-time.

Fitzgerald replaced Noel Kennelly in the 28th minute and made a valuable contribution to Kerry's drive for victory when he moved outfield in the second half.

Liam Hassett extended Kerry lead shortly after the re-start, but Galway stormed back into the game with points from Michael Donnellan, Tommie Joyce, Pádraic Joyce and Seán Óg de Paor to move ahead of the Munster champions.

It was Galway's most positive phase.

With Fitzgerald controlling matters away from the full-forward line, it was only a matter of time before Kerry made their possession count on the scoreboard.

Fitzgerald supplied the in-form Liam Hassett for his third point from play but Niall Finnegan responded with a pointed free for Galway.

Fitzgerald again caught Martin McNamara's kick-out and raced through to land a point; Russell and the hard-working Aodán Mac Gearailt then added a point each to push Kerry four points clear and within sight of the finishing line.

Substitute Shay Walsh narrowed the margin with a point from play coming up to full-time but the ever-dangerous Crowley, who had landed the opening score of the game, had the honour of kicking the final point of the 2000 final as Kerry, despite hitting sixteen wides, claimed victory by 0-17 to 1-10.

Kerry's captain, Seamus Moynihan

2000 ALL-IRELAND
SENIOR FOOTBALL CHAMPIONSHIP FINAL REPLAY

SCORERS – KERRY: Dara Ó Cinnéide 0-4; Johnny Crowley 0-3; Liam Hassett 0-3; Mike Frank Russell 0-2; Aodán Mac Gearailt 0-2; Noel Kennelly 0-1; Maurice Fitzgerald 0-1; Eamonn Fitzmaurice 0-1

SCORERS – GALWAY: Declan Meehan 1-0; Niall Finnegan 0-2; Michael Donnellan 0-2; Kevin Walsh 0-1; Seán Óg de Paor 0-1; Pádraic Joyce 0-1; Tommie Joyce 0-1; Joe Bergin 0-1; Shay Walsh 0-1

KERRY

Declan O'Keeffe

Mike Hassett	Séamus Moynihan *(Captain)*	Mike McCarthy
Tomás Ó Sé	Tom O'Sullivan	Eamonn Fitzmaurice

Darragh Ó Sé   Donal Daly

Aodán Mac Gearailt	Liam Hassett	Noel Kennelly
Mike Frank Russell	Dara Ó Cinnéide	Johnny Crowley

SUBSTITUTES: Maurice Fitzgerald for Noel Kennelly; Tommy Griffin for Tom O'Sullivan

GALWAY

Martin McNamara

Tomás Meehan	Gary Fahey	Richie Fahey
Declan Meehan	John Divilly	Seán Óg de Paor

Kevin Walsh   Seán Ó Dómhnaill

Paul Clancy	Michael Donnellan	Tommie Joyce
Derek Savage	Pádraic Joyce *(Captain)*	Niall Finnegan

SUBSTITUTES: Joe Bergin for Kevin Walsh; Kevin Walsh for Seán Ó Domhnaill; John Donnellan for Tommie Joyce; Shay Walsh for Paul Clancy

KERRY – 2000 (REPLAY)

Back row, left to right: Darragh Ó Sé, Noel Kennelly, Tom O'Sullivan, Mike Hassett,
Liam Hassett, Donal Daly, Johnny Crowley, Aodán Mac Gearailt
Front row, left to right: Eamonn Fitzmaurice, Mike Frank Russell, Dara Ó Cinnéide,
Séamus Moynihan, Declan O'Keeffe, Tomás Ó Sé, Mike McCarthy

Kerry manager, Páidí Ó Sé

48

Declan O'Keeffe
(Kerry) 2nd

Kieran McKeever
(Derry) 1st

Séamus Moynihan
(Kerry) 2nd

Mike McCarthy
(Kerry) 1st

Declan Meehan
(Galway) 1st

Kieran McGeeney
(Armagh) 2nd

Anthony Rainbow
(Kildare) 1st

Anthony Tohill
(Derry) 4th

Darragh Ó Sé
(Kerry) 1st

Michael Donnellan
(Galway) 2nd

Liam Hassett
(Kerry) 1st

Oisín McConville
(Armagh) 1st

Mike Frank Russell
(Kerry) 1st

Pádraic Joyce
(Galway) 2nd

Derek Savage
(Galway) 1st

2001 ALL–IRELAND FOOTBALL FINAL

SUNDAY, SEPTEMBER 23

GALWAY VERSUS MEATH

CROKE PARK

REFEREE: MICHAEL COLLINS (CORK)

GALWAY 0-17   MEATH 0-8

Galway footballers turned in a quite exceptional performance to overcome Meath by 9 points – a victory that was all the more significant considering John O'Mahony's side had lost to Roscommon in the Connacht semi-final.

That defeat was but a distant memory as Galway powered past favourites Meath with a superb display to claim their 9th All-Ireland title.

Pádraic Joyce epitomised the Galway spirit more than anyone else.

The Killererin club-man untypically kicked a number of wides in the opening half, but regained his composure after the break with devastating effect.

Joyce took full advantage of weaknesses in the Meath defence and scored a massive 9 point total in the second half alone, including five from play.

Declan Meehan was outstanding from start to finish and his darting runs caused added problems for an already pressurised Meath back line.

Kevin Walsh produced another top-class display while Tomás Mannion was a rock in defence and thwarted many a Meath attack.

Every Galway player made a very significant contribution to what was a famous victory, achieved with style and authority.

It was a momentous end to a campaign that saw Galway beat Leitrim; then lose to Roscommon, before turning their season around with victories over Wicklow, Armagh, Cork, Roscommon, Derry and Meath, in the final itself.

In stark contrast to the All-Ireland semi-final, when Meath brushed Kerry aside, nothing went right for the Leinster champions on this occasion.

To compound Meath's problems, their player of the championship, Ollie Murphy suffered a broken hand in the 41st minute and was replaced three minutes later by Paddy Reynolds while Nigel Nestor was dismissed on a second yellow in the 50th minute.

True to form, Meath continued to battle on but the absence of Murphy and Nestor had a serious impact on their challenge.

Moreover, Meath's last chance of salvaging the game was lost when Trevor Giles shot wide from a penalty in the 59th minute when a goal would have reduced the margin to just two points.

Galway failed to convert their chances in the opening half as the sides finished level, 0-6 each at the break but the game changed utterly after the re-start.

Joyce and Evan Kelly swapped points early in the second half but Meath then suffered a setback when Murphy had to retire injured.

Joyce then proceeded to take control and kicked over five points, including three from play.

Substitute John Cullinane replied with a point for Meath but another Joyce score made it 0-13 to 0-8 in Galway's favour.

Then came the Giles' penalty miss and Galway took complete control thereafter as Joyce scored two more points to bring his match tally to 0-10.

Paul Clancy tacked on a point and the brilliant Meehan, who was denied a goal earlier through a superb save by Meath goalkeeper Cormac Sullivan, deservedly got his name on the scoresheet.

Dual star, Alan Kerins, who was on the losing Galway team in the All-Ireland hurling final two weeks earlier, came on as a substitute in injury-time along with Kieran Comer.

Galway captain, Gary Fahey

SCORERS – GALWAY: Pádraic Joyce 0-10; Paul Clancy 0-2; Joe Bergin 0-2; Michael Donnellan 0-1; Ja Fallon 0-1; Declan Meehan 0-1

SCORERS – MEATH: Ray Magee 0-2; Nigel Crawford 0-1; John McDermott 0-1; Evan Kelly 0-1; Trevor Giles 0-1; Ollie Murphy 0-1; John Cullinane 0-1

GALWAY

Alan Keane

Kieran Fitzgerald   Gary Fahey *(Captain)*   Richie Fahey

Declan Meehan   Tomás Mannion   Seán Óg de Paor

Kevin Walsh   Michael Donnellan

Joe Bergin   Paul Clancy   Ja Fallon

Derek Savage   Pádraic Joyce   Tommie Joyce

SUBSTITUTES: Alan Kerins for Joe Bergin; Kieran Comer for Tommie Joyce

MEATH

Cormac Sullivan

Mark O'Reilly   Darren Fay *(Captain)*   Cormac Murphy

Donal Curtis   Hank Traynor   Nigel Nestor

Nigel Crawford   John McDermott

Evan Kelly   Trevor Giles   Richie Kealy

Ollie Murphy   Graham Geraghty   Ray Magee

SUBSTITUTES: Paddy Reynolds for Ollie Murphy; John Cullinane for Richie Kealy; Niall Kelly for Cormac Murphy; Adrian Kenny for Ray Magee

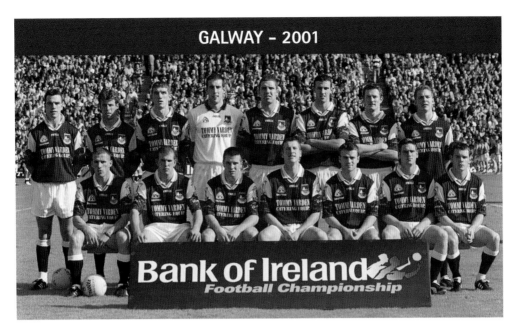

GALWAY - 2001

Back row, left to right: Pádraic Joyce, Tomás Mannion, Kieran Fitzgerald,
Alan Keane, Kevin Walsh, Joe Bergin, Ja Fallon, Michael Donnellan
Front row, left: Seán Óg de Paor, Richie Fahey, Tommie Joyce, Gary Fahey,
Derek Savage, Paul Clancy, Declan Meehan

Galway manager, John O'Mahony

2001 ALL-STARS FOOTBALL SELECTION

Cormac Sullivan
(Meath) 1st

Kieran Fitzgerald
(Galway) 1st

Darren Fay
(Meath) 3rd

Coman Goggins
(Dublin) 1st

Declan Meehan
(Galway) 2nd

Francie Grehan
(Roscommon) 1st

Seán Óg de Paor
(Galway) 2nd

Kevin Walsh
(Galway) 2nd

Rory O'Connell
(Westmeath) 1st

Evan Kelly
(Meath) 1st

Stephen O'Neill
(Tyrone) 1st

Michael Donnellan
(Galway) 3rd

Ollie Murphy
(Meath) 2nd

Pádraic Joyce
(Galway) 3rd

Johnny Crowley
(Kerry) 1st

2002
ALL–IRELAND
FOOTBALL FINAL

SUNDAY, SEPTEMBER 22

ARMAGH VERSUS KERRY

CROKE PARK

REFEREE: JOHN BANNON
(LONGFORD)

ARMAGH 1–12 KERRY 0–14

The sight of Kieran McGeeney sinking to his knees at the final whistle is a memory that Armagh football followers will cherish forever.

It was a precious moment in time that signified the culmination of a lifetime of hopes and dreams for every single player that ever wore the famous orange and white jersey.

McGeeney's spontaneous reaction to the sound of the final whistle, more than anything else, encapsulated the magnitude of the achievement of a truly superb team that delivered an All-Ireland senior football title to the county for the very first time.

McGeeney, once again, provided the leadership and inspiration as the Ulster champions came from four points behind at the break to outscore favourites Kerry by 1-5 to 0-3 in the second half.

Still, Kerry held a four points advantage entering the final quarter when the vital score arrived courtesy of Oisín McConville, who underlined his class following a disappointing opening half in which he not only failed to score, but also had his penalty kick saved by Declan O'Keeffe.

McConville, who had converted a free and a '45 during the third quarter, raced on to a flicked return pass from Paul McGrane and the whole of Armagh held its breath as his intent became apparent.

The Crossmaglen player kept his composure and drove the ball into the corner of the net past O'Keeffe to narrow the deficit to a single point.

The impressive Ronan Clarke then levelled the match for the fifth time before Steven McDonnell kicked over the lead point, which as it transpired turned out to be the winning score.

By that stage, Armagh were in control and Kerry, aided by the breeze, were unable to respond, which was in stark contrast to the first half when the team played with confidence to put them in a strong position at half-time.

Armagh improved beyond recognition after the break and credit must be given to their manager, Joe Kernan who got his players in the right frame of mind for the second half challenge.

The Armagh players displayed true grit and determination after the break and pinned Kerry back in their own half while restricting their attack to just three points in total, but tellingly only one from play, which was scored by Liam Hassett.

The sides were level on three occasions in the opening 15 minutes during which all 8 points came from play.

Steven McDonnell and Ronan Clarke scored two apiece for Armagh while Mike Frank Russell landed two for Kerry with one each coming from Eoin Brosnan and Colm Cooper.

John McEntee edged Armagh ahead with a point from play but had to retire in the 24th minute with concussion.

Donal Daly and Darragh Ó Sé won a plentiful supply of ball at midfield and the Kerry attack prospered against an overstretched Armagh defence.

Dara Ó Cinnéide kicked two points in quick succession to ease Kerry ahead for the first time in the 21st minute while Russell came close to scoring a goal but his shot came off McGeeney for a point.

Even though Diarmaid Marsden sent over a point from play, there was still no respite for Armagh.

Eoin Brosnan flashed a goal bound shot narrowly wide of the Armagh post as Kerry threatened to overrun the Ulster champions.

Ó Cinnéide and Cooper tacked on a point each as Kerry continued to play with a confidence that was reflected in their 0-11 to 0-6 lead.

Armagh were presented with a glorious opportunity to reverse the trend when Oisín McConville was fouled just before half-time and referee John Bannon awarded a penalty.

McConville took the kick, but his shot to the corner was well blocked by Kerry keeper, O'Keeffe.

Although Marsden kicked his second point in injury-time, Armagh still trailed at the break by four points, 0-11 to 0-7, and significantly had to face a stiff breeze in the second half.

The Kerry players were on the field for some minutes before Armagh re-appeared.

Kerry shot a number of wides from scorable positions, at the start of the second half, before Armagh, inspired by McGeeney, took control.

McGrane, John Toal and Andrew McCann also stamped their authority on the game while Clarke, Marsden and McDonnell tormented the Kerry backs.

Marsden and Hassett scored the only points from play in the third-quarter – a period which also yielded two points apiece from free takers Ó Cinnéide and McConville.

Then in the 55th minute, McConville's shot found the corner of the net to rock Kerry and give Armagh real impetus at a critical phase of the game.

Clarke and McDonnell then kicked over a point each and one sensed that the Sam Maguire Cup would be heading to the Orchard County for the very first time.

Armagh battled like men possessed in the closing ten minutes and all the years of heartbreak and disappointment were washed away when the final whistle sounded and McGeeney fell to his knees in thanks with the match ball close to his heart.

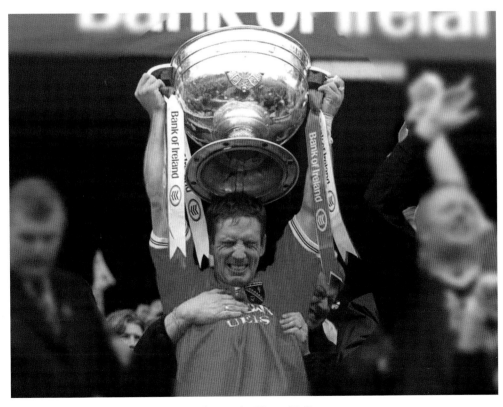

Armagh captain, Kieran McGeeney

2002 ALL–IRELAND
SENIOR FOOTBALL CHAMPIONSHIP FINAL

SCORERS – ARMAGH: Oisín McConville 1-2; Steven McDonnell 0-3;
Ronan Clarke 0-3; Diarmaid Marsden 0-3; John McEntee 0-1

SCORERS – KERRY: Dara Ó Cinnéide 0-5; Mike Frank Russell 0-3;
Colm Cooper 0-2; Liam Hassett 0-2; Eoin Brosnan 0-1;
Eamonn Fitzmaurice 0-1

ARMAGH
Benny Tierney

Enda McNulty	Justin McNulty	Francie Bellew
Aidan O'Rourke	Kieran McGeeney *(Captain)*	Andrew McCann

John Toal   Paul McGrane

Paddy McKeever	John McEntee	Oisín McConville
Steven McDonnell	Ronan Clarke	Diarmaid Marsden

SUBSTITUTES: Barry O'Hagan for John McEntee; Tony McEntee for Paddy McKeever

KERRY
Declan O'Keeffe

Marc Ó Sé	Séamus Moynihan	Mike McCarthy
Tomás Ó Sé	Eamonn Fitzmaurice	John Sheehan

Darragh Ó Sé *(Captain)*   Donal Daly

Seán Ó Sullivan	Eoin Brosnan	Liam Hassett
Mike Frank Russell	Dara Ó Cinnéide	Colm Cooper

SUBSTITUTES: Aodán Mac Gearailt for Seán O'Sullivan; Tom O'Sullivan for Marc Ó Sé;
Johnny Crowley for Liam Hassett; Barry O'Shea for Donal Daly

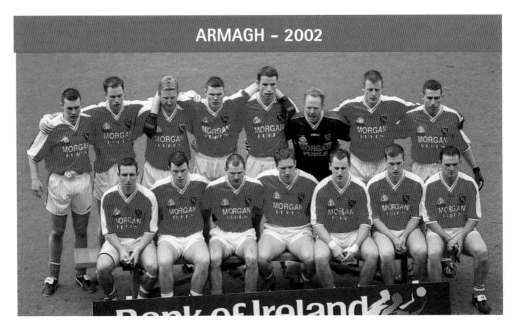

Back row, left to right: Oisín McConville, Andrew McCann, Francie Bellew,
John Toal, Paul McGrane, Benny Tierney, Justin McNulty, Diarmaid Marsden
Front row, left to right: Enda McNulty, Ronan Clarke, Steven McDonnell,
Kieran McGeeney, Paddy McKeever, John McEntee, Aidan O'Rourke

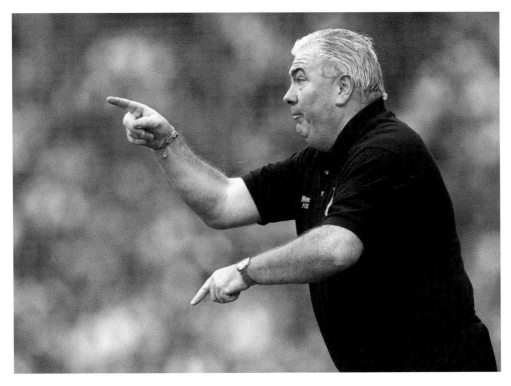

Armagh manager, Joe Kernan

2002 ALL-STARS FOOTBALL SELECTION

Stephen Cluxton
(Dublin) 1st

Enda McNulty
(Armagh) 1st

Paddy Christie
(Dublin) 1st

Anthony Lynch
(Cork) 2nd

Aidan O'Rourke
(Armagh) 1st

Kieran McGeeney
(Armagh) 3rd

Kevin Cassidy
(Donegal) 1st

Darragh Ó Sé
(Kerry) 2nd

Paul McGrane
(Armagh) 1st

Steven McDonnell
(Armagh) 1st

Eamonn O'Hara
(Sligo) 1st

Oisín McConville
(Armagh) 2nd

Peter Canavan
(Tyrone) 4th

Ray Cosgrove
(Dublin) 1st

Colm Cooper
(Kerry) 1st

2003
ALL-IRELAND
FOOTBALL FINAL

SUNDAY, SEPTEMBER 28

TYRONE VERSUS ARMAGH

CROKE PARK

REFEREE: BRIAN WHITE
(WEXFORD)

TYRONE 0- 12 ARMAGH 0-9

There were scenes of unrestrained delight when Peter Canavan raised the Sam Maguire Cup on the Hogan Stand following Tyrone's 0-12 to 0-9 victory over the 2002 champions Armagh.

It was a first ever All-Ireland senior title for Tyrone and hordes of their devoted followers raced on to the pitch at the finish to show their appreciation to a group of players and management that had created history.

It was no wonder that Canavan, a footballing genius, was the centre of attention.

There was major concern about Canavan's fitness coming into the All-Ireland final following a serious ankle injury sustained early on in the semi-final win over Kerry.

It was nothing short of miraculous that he was able to play any part given that he damaged his ankle again during training on the Thursday week before the final.

But, despite being clearly hampered by injury, Canavan led the team out to a thunderous reception and played through the pain barrier in the opening half, during which he kicked five points from frees and laid the foundation for ultimate glory.

His influence in the first half of a rugged encounter was inestimable as Tyrone moved 0-8 to 0-4 ahead by half-time, with the energetic and hard-working Enda McGinley landing the last score before the break.

Indeed, McGinley looked odds on to score a goal, but his powerful shot was brilliantly deflected over the crossbar by Armagh goalkeeper, Paul Hearty.

Canavan was forced to retire at half-time but in a pre-planned move, Tyrone manager, Mickey Harte, who stamped his imprint on the team, sent his captain back on in the closing minutes to steady the ship and guide his young team to a historic victory.

It worked to perfection and the final whistle signalled the end of a lifetime of heartbreak and disappointment for Tyrone supporters who had despaired of such a momentous day ever arriving.

The game itself was a tough, bruising encounter as both teams competed ferociously.

Cormac McAnallen was highly effective at full-back for a strong-running and well-structured Tyrone side that settled to their task with confidence.

Space was at a premium and defences coped exceedingly well under pressure against some of the most lethal forwards in the game.

One of those outstanding attackers, Armagh's Steven McDonnell was denied a certain goal in the 68th minute by a magnificent block from Conor Gormley that in all probability decided the destination of the Sam Maguire Cup.

It was the defining moment in a game that Tyrone deserved to win but in which resilient Armagh remained in contention right to the very finish.

If McDonnell, who was a constant threat and contributed two points from play, had scored a goal at that critical stage, 14-man Armagh may well have gone on to retain the title with a late rally.

Gormley's bravery and skill in making the block will assuredly warrant special mention whenever and wherever the 2003 All-Ireland Football Final is being discussed.

Midfielders Kevin Hughes and Seán Cavanagh, defender Philip Jordan and play-anywhere Brian Dooher produced top-notch displays, but there were valuable contributions also from every single Tyrone player, most especially substitute Stephen O'Neill, who replaced flu-victim, Brian McGuigan just before half-time, and scored two points from play.

Significantly, McGuigan returned to the action at the start of the second half for Canavan and proceeded to play a crucial part in Tyrone's march to victory.

And Canavan's former pupil, Owen Mulligan, had a hard physical confrontation with Francie Bellew all through but still managed to raise his game when the need was greatest and converted two rather difficult free kicks.

Canavan landed the opening score with a pointed free in the early exchanges but John McEntee from play soon levelled the match.

It was to be the only time the sides were level in the entire game.

Gerard Cavlan sent over a fine point from play and Tyrone never relinquished the lead thereafter.

Canavan stretched Tyrone's advantage with two further points from frees and the Ulster champions moved 0-5 to 0-1 ahead following a McGuigan point from play.

Cavanagh had a golden chance of a goal in the 19th minute but his left-footed shot screamed wide.

Earlier, in the 5th minute, Armagh forward Diarmaid Marsden, put through by Oisín McConville, missed an opportunity when a goal appeared the certain outcome.

Marsden, an exceptionally gifted player, suffered a head injury in the 25th minute and was replaced by Paddy McKeever.

Marsden returned to the fray in the 50th minute, kicked a point, and was then red-carded following a clash with Philip Jordan who ran straight into him.

(Marsden was later exonerated on appeal to the Central Council)

The dismissal of Marsden, after the referee consulted with an umpire, represented a huge setback for Armagh, who clearly missed his influence in the dramatic final quarter, during which Kieran McGeeney, Paul McGrane, McConville and McDonnell took the fight to Tyrone.

Cavlan's goal attempt early in the second half was narrowly off target as Tyrone continued to create openings with sharp incisive attacks.

Impressive Armagh substitute, Paddy McKeever kicked the opening point of the second half from a free but Mulligan replied with his first score of the game.

McKeever pointed his second free and Marsden tacked on a point from play before Mulligan kept his composure under pressure to kick over a free.

But just as the game reached a new level of intensity, Marsden was controversially sent-off and one sensed it was not going to be Armagh's day.

There were some bone-crushing tackles in the closing 10 minutes as both sides endeavoured to gain supremacy.

McConville and Stephen O'Neill exchanged points; Canavan re-entered the game to a rapturous reception; Conor Gormley made an indelible imprint on the game with a perfectly timed tackle on McDonnell while O'Neill capped a fine individual display with his second point from play.

Ironically, Tyrone finished with a tally of 0-12, the same total as in their last All-Ireland final appearance in 1995 when the county lost to Dublin by a point, 1-10 to 0-12, on a day when Canavan scored 11 points.

But thoughts of 1995 were far from Canavan's mind when the final whistle sounded in the 2003 final and he knew that, at long last, his lifelong dream had been realised as Tyrone became the 19th county to win the All-Ireland senior football title.

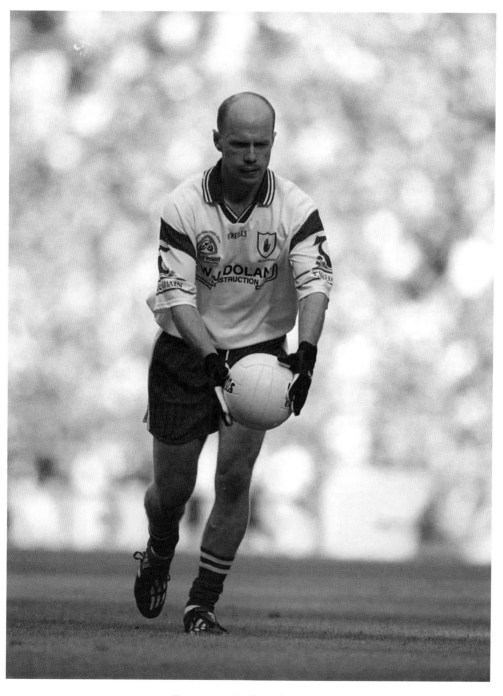

Tyrone captain, Peter Canavan

2003 ALL-IRELAND
SENIOR FOOTBALL CHAMPIONSHIP FINAL

SCORERS – TYRONE: Peter Canavan 0-5; Stephen O'Neill 0-2; Owen Mulligan 0-2;
Enda McGinley 0-1; Gerard Cavlan 0-1; Brian McGuigan 0-1

SCORERS – ARMAGH: Oisín McConville 0-3; Steven McDonnell 0-2;
Paddy McKeever 0-2; Diarmaid Marsden 0-1;
John McEntee 0-1

TYRONE

John Devine

Ciarán Gourley   Cormac McAnallen   Ryan McMenamin

Conor Gormley   Gavin Devlin   Philip Jordan

Kevin Hughes   Seán Cavanagh

Brian Dooher   Brian McGuigan   Gerald Cavlan

Enda McGinley   Peter Canavan *(Captain)*   Owen Mulligan

SUBSTITUTES: Stephen O'Neill for Brian McGuigan;
Brian McGuigan for Peter Canavan; Colin Holmes for Ciarán Gourley;
Peter Canavan for Gerard Cavlan; Chris Lawn for Conor Gormley

ARMAGH

Paul Hearty

Francie Bellew   Enda McNulty   Andy Mallon

Aidan O'Rourke   Kieran McGeeney *(Captain)*   Andrew McCann

Tony McEntee   Paul McGrane

Philip Loughran   John McEntee   Oisín McConville

Ronan Clarke   Steven McDonnell   Diarmaid Marsden

SUBSTITUTES: Paddy McKeever for Diarmaid Marsden;
Kieran Hughes for Andy Mallon;
Diarmaid Marsden for Ronan Clarke; Barry O'Hagan for John McEntee

TYRONE – 2003

Back row, left to right: Peter Loughran, Seán Cavanagh, Cormac McAnallen, John Devine, Pascal McConnell, Enda McGinley, Mickey Coleman, Owen Mulligan, Philip Jordan, Brian McGuigan, Kevin Hughes, Stephen O'Neill, Gerard Cavlan, Gavin Devlin
Front row, left to right: Michael McGee, Chris Lawn, Brian Robinson, Cormac McGinley, Ciarán Gourley, Dermot Carlin, Peter Canavan, Ryan McMenamin, Brian Dooher, Declan McCrossan, Frank McGuigan, Mark Harte, Ryan Mellon, Séamus Mulgrew, Conor Gormley

Tyrone manager, Mickey Harte

2003 ALL-STARS FOOTBALL SELECTION

Fergal Byron
(Laois) 1st

Francie Bellew
(Armagh) 1st

Cormac McAnallen
(Tyrone) 1st

Joe Higgins
(Laois) 1st

Conor Gormley
(Tyrone) 1st

Tom Kelly
(Laois) 1st

Philip Jordan
(Tyrone) 1st

Kevin Walsh
(Galway) 3rd

Seán Cavanagh
(Tyrone) 1st

Brian Dooher
(Tyrone) 1st

Brian McGuigan
(Tyrone) 1st

Declan Browne
(Tipperary) 2nd

Steven McDonnell
(Armagh) 2nd

Peter Canavan
(Tyrone) 5th

Adrian Sweeney
(Donegal) 1st

2004
ALL-IRELAND
FOOTBALL FINAL

SUNDAY, SEPTEMBER 26

KERRY VERSUS MAYO

CROKE PARK

REFEREE: PAT McENANEY
(MONAGHAN)

KERRY 1- 20 MAYO 2-9

Kerry claimed their 33rd All-Ireland title with a comprehensive 8 points victory over a Mayo side that were simply unable to raise their standard to meet the awesome challenge.

Kerry took control at midfield and other crucial areas from the very start and never once relinquished their grip with a display of pace and skill that overwhelmed an out-of-sorts Mayo.

Kerry were much sharper to the breaking ball and, despite the fillip of a 5th minute goal from Alan Dillon, it became increasingly evident that Mayo were simply unable to cope with the pressure being applied from all sectors by the rampant Munster Champions.

Such was Kerry's dominance from the second quarter onwards, it was apparent that Mayo were going to struggle to mount a serious challenge.

Ciarán McDonald kicked over a wonderful long-range point from the right wing, which preceded Dillon's goal, but that was about as good as it got for a struggling Mayo.

McDonald, who scored three points, showed flashes of his undoubted genius throughout but, as the game wore on and as Kerry became more dominant, the brilliant Crossmolina clubman had to move further and further outfield to gain even limited possession.

William Kirby was magnificent at midfield for Kerry and scored three points from play while Johnny Crowley produced a creative display that helped pave the way for victory.

Crowley used his strength and experience as the target man to win vital possession and linked up with the outstanding Colm Cooper, who scored 1-5 while team captain, Dara Ó Cinnéide, contributed 8 points in a highly impressive display.

Wing-back, Tomás Ó Sé was another star performer on a day when Kerry dictated the play as Mayo struggled to make any real impact.

Kerry goalkeeper, Diarmuid Murphy could not be faulted for the two Mayo goals and embellished a superb display with excellent saves from Michael Conroy and Trevor Mortimer.

Mike McCarthy, Aidan O'Mahony, Tom O'Sullivan, Marc Ó Sé and Eamonn Fitzmaurice proved to be a strong defensive unit and more than played their part in Kerry's victory.

Fitzmaurice had the difficult task of trying to curb McDonald but the Finuge player fared well against Mayo's most dangerous forward.

Kirby's midfield partner Eoin Brosnan was also highly effective and largely controlled that vital sector against Fergal Kelly and Ronan McGarrity.

David Brady added strength to the sector when introduced in place of Kelly in the 23rd minute, but there was simply no stopping Kirby and Brosnan.

Paul Galvin impressed greatly with his strong running and scored a point for good measure.

Declan O'Sullivan, too, kicked over a point from play while his work-rate and general play were significant factors in Kerry's overall team effort.

Liam Hassett worked tirelessly and had a right battle with one of Mayo's best defenders Peadar Gardiner, who tried with all his might to stem the tide.

Darragh Ó Sé missed the final because of injury while Séamus Moynihan and Mike Frank Russell both came off the bench in the closing stages.

The crucial score came in the 25th minute when Cooper scored a magnificent goal to push Kerry 7 points clear, 1-10 to 1-3.

It could have been even worse for Mayo only that Crowley was denied a goal by goalkeeper, Peter Burke, who brought off a magnificent save.

Cooper hit 1-2 from play in the opening half while Marc Ó Sé, Kirby and Declan O'Sullivan each sent over a point from play as Kerry played with total confidence.

Ó Cinnéide converted a '45 before half-time to bring his tally to seven points - two from play – and leave Kerry comfortably ahead at the break by 1-12 to 1-4.

Mayo had scored 1-2 of their first half total by the 11th minute and could only accumulate two points from frees for the remainder of the half from McDonald – a superb point with the outside of his boot – and one from Dillon.

Conor Mortimer shot over the bar with a goal chance on early in the second half but any remote chance of a Mayo revival was dashed when Kirby, Cooper and Ó Cinnéide landed a point apiece to continue Kerry's dominance.

Kerry had surged 11 points clear by the 48th minute, 1-16 to 1-5, and the game was over as a contest when impressive substitute, Michael Conroy scored a late goal for the Connacht champions.

It was a special victory for Kerry and their proud captain, Dara Ó Cinnéide from An Ghaeltacht, who raised the Sam Maguire Cup like his clubman and former county manager, Páidí Ó Sé some 19 years earlier.

Kerry captain, Dara Ó Cinnéide

SCORERS – KERRY: Dara Ó Cinnéide 0-8; Colm Cooper 1-5; William Kirby 0-3; Declan O'Sullivan 0-1; Mike Frank Russell 0-1; Paul Galvin 0-1; Marc Ó Sé 0-1

SCORERS – MAYO: Alan Dillon 1-2; Michael Conroy 1-1; Ciarán McDonald 0-3; Brian Maloney 0-1; Andy Moran 0-1; Conor Mortimer 0-1

KERRY

Diarmuid Murphy

Aidan O'Mahony   Mike McCarthy   Tom O'Sullivan

Marc Ó Sé   Eamonn Fitzmaurice   Tomás Ó Sé

Eoin Brosnan   William Kirby

Liam Hassett   Declan O'Sullivan   Paul Galvin

Colm Cooper   Dara Ó Cinnéide *(Captain)*   Johnny Crowley

SUBSTITUTES: Séamus Moynihan for Liam Hassett; Mike Frank Russell for Johnny Crowley; Ronan O'Connor for Dara Ó Cinnéide; Paddy Kelly for Paul Galvin; Brendan Guiney for Tomás Ó Sé

MAYO

Peter Burke

Dermot Geraghty   David Heaney   Gary Ruane *(Captain)*

Peadar Gardiner   James Nallen   Pat Kelly

Ronan McGarrity   Fergal Kelly

Trevor Mortimer   Ciarán McDonald   Brian Maloney

Conor Mortimer   James Gill   Alan Dillon

SUBSTITUTES: David Brady for Fergal Kelly; Conor Moran for Dermot Geraghty; Michael Conroy for James Gill; Andy Moran for Conor Mortimer; Paddy Navin for David Heaney

Back row, left to right: Tommy Griffin, Mike Quirke, John Cronin, Bryan Sheehan,
Ronan O'Connor, Johnny Crowley, Marc Ó Sé, Tom O'Sullivan, Diarmuid Murphy, Liam Hassett,
Mike McCarthy, Paddy Kelly, John Sheehan, Declan Quill, William Kirby, Ronán Ó Flatharta
Front row, left to right: Brendan Guiney, Seán O'Sullivan, Noel Kennelly, Eamonn Fitzmaurice,
Paul Galvin, Declan O'Sullivan, Dara Ó Cinnéide, Tomás Ó Sé, Colm Cooper, Aidan O'Mahony,
Eoin Brosnan, Kieran Cremin, Mike Frank Russell

Kerry manager, Jack O'Connor

Diarmuid Murphy
(Kerry) 1st

Tom O'Sullivan
(Kerry) 1st

Barry Owens
(Fermanagh) 1st

Mike McCarthy
(Kerry) 2nd

Tomás Ó Sé
(Kerry) 1st

James Nallen
(Mayo) 2nd

John Keane
(Westmeath) 1st

Marty McGrath
(Fermanagh) 1st

Seán Cavanagh
(Tyrone) 2nd

Paul Galvin
(Kerry) 1st

Ciarán McDonald
(Mayo) 1st

Dessie Dolan
(Westmeath) 1st

Colm Cooper
(Kerry) 2nd

Enda Muldoon
(Derry) 1st

Matty Forde
(Wexford) 1st

2005
ALL–IRELAND
FOOTBALL FINAL

SUNDAY, SEPTEMBER 25

TYRONE VERSUS KERRY

CROKE PARK

REFEREE: MICHAEL MONAHAN
(KILDARE)

TYRONE 1-16 KERRY 2-10

Tyrone delivered a commanding all-action display to claim their second All-Ireland title in three years with a more resounding victory over Kerry than the three points victory would signify.

Tyrone's victory was in itself a statement of defiance against the 'old order' and verification that Mickey Harte's side had raised the bar to such a level that even a highly-motivated traditional power like Kerry could not overcome the challenge.

Tyrone played with such self-belief and confidence, once they established their rhythm, that the result was hardly ever in doubt, despite the fact that a courageous Kerry team kept the game ultra-competitive right to the final whistle.

Tyrone looked so fresh and full of running at the finish that it was difficult to comprehend that it was their 10th game in Championship 2005, which included three teak-tough contests against arch Ulster rivals Armagh.

Kerry matched Tyrone's intensity for long stages but were simply unable to sustain the herculean effort for the entire duration of the game.

Kerry faced a team that had perfected the art of total football and came off second best after a magnificent opening, during which Colm Cooper was superb.

But as the game unfolded and Tyrone applied severe pressure, Kerry players failed to release the ball quickly enough and were often caught in possession or gave away unnecessary frees.

Cooper picked up an injury off the ball in the 9th minute, which appeared to affect the overall balance of the Kerry team, who were very reliant all season on the Dr. Crokes club man.

It took some time for Cooper to recover from the effects of the facial blow but gradually he began to exert his influence again and finished as Kerry's top scorer with five points.

Television pictures failed to pick out the Tyrone player that made contact with Cooper; neither did any of the umpires witness the incident.

Peter Canavan left his indelible imprint on the final with a masterly taken goal and a superb point from play.

Canavan expertly finished the ball to the next in the 36th minute for what proved to be the most crucial score of the match.

Owen Mulligan collected a high ball from Philip Jordan under pressure from Paul Galvin, who was left isolated in the full-back position.

Mulligan showed commendable strength and composure to lay it off to his former teacher, who neatly placed the ball in the corner of the net, despite the valiant effort of goalkeeper, Diarmuid Murphy.

As it transpired, it was the only goal Tyrone scored in the final, but what a memorable one – and furthermore it was the only goal that Murphy conceded in the 2005 Championship.

Canavan, who had struggled with injury all season, took a break after half-time but re-entered the fray to a rapturous reception with 15 minutes remaining.

The former, 'Footballer of the Year', then proceeded to score an audacious point, which steadied Tyrone, who were struggling to regain the initiative following a great goal from Tomás Ó Sé.

Canavan later announced his retirement from an inter-county football career that marked him out as a rare and wonderful talent with extraordinary leadership qualities.

The 2005 final began at a frantic pace and within 90 seconds, Cooper, despite the close attention of Ryan McMenamin, lofted the ball over the bar after running on to a free kick by William Kirby.

Eoin Brosnan then landed a fine point from play as Kerry settled to their task with commendable style and vigour.

Ryan Mellon responded with a point for Tyrone in the 5th minute and the same player then levelled the match with another excellent effort from play.

Kerry struck for the opening goal in the 7th minute when Cooper hand passed over the head of Michael McGee to the onrushing Dara Ó Cinnéide who superbly finished the ball to the net.

Owen Mulligan responded almost immediately with a point from play but, at that juncture, Kerry held the upperhand with Declan O'Sullivan winning an abundance of possession out field.

Tyrone defender, Conor Gormley proved highly effective at cutting off the supply of ball to the Kerry inside forward line, as Tyrone slowly but surely stamped their authority on the game.

Brosnan extended Kerry's lead with a point from play and the impressive Brian McGuigan hit the side netting with a goal chance on.

Mulligan then converted a free in the 21st minute.

Tyrone were now in full flight as McGuigan and Brian Dooher landed spectacular points from play while Stephen O'Neill, from a free, edged Tyrone ahead for the very first time in the 31st minute.

Cooper replied with a point from play – Kerry's first score for 16 minutes – before the game took a decisive twist in injury-time.

Mulligan gathered a high ball from Jordan, held off Galvin and laid on the pass for Canavan, who expertly steered the ball to the net.

Darragh Ó Sé kicked a fine point from play to narrow the margin to just three points at the break, Tyrone 1-8, Kerry 1-5.

Canavan was replaced by Colin Holmes at the start of the second half, which began with early points from Cooper and Mulligan.

McMenamin, Gormley and Jordan continued to perform at a high level in defence for the Ulster side.

All three won a share of possession and set up a series of attacks.

Davy Harte, Michael McGee and Joe McMahon, until substituted because of injury, also worked tirelessly throughout and made valuable contributions to Tyrone's victory.

After a quiet opening half, Seán Cavanagh began to dictate play around midfield and run at a Kerry defence, now experiencing serious difficulties, notwithstanding the firm resistance provided by Tomás Ó Sé.

Stephen O'Neill sent over two splendid points from play while substitute Chris Lawn, who replaced the injured Joe McMahon, cleared his lines with confidence and proved a steadying influence in the closing stages.

Cooper continued to be the main threat in the Kerry forward line and was well supported by his Dr. Crokes club mate, Eoin Brosnan.

Darragh Ó Sé kicked his second point from play in the 53rd minute while his younger brother, Tomás scored a superb goal to reduce the deficit to a single point.

Darragh Ó Sé then missed an opportunity to level the match when his attempted point effort drifted wide.

By now Canavan was back on the field of play and he steadied Tyrone with a point from play from a very tight angle while Cooper and O'Neill exchanged points from frees as the pressure mounted.

Cooper sent over a free in the 64th minute for what proved to be Kerry's last score as Tyrone stormed back with clinching scores from McGuigan and Jordan.

There was so much raw emotion at the finish as inspirational Tyrone manager, Mickey Harte and his players paid heartfelt tributes to their late-lamented captain, Cormac McAnallen, who sadly died on March 2nd 2004.

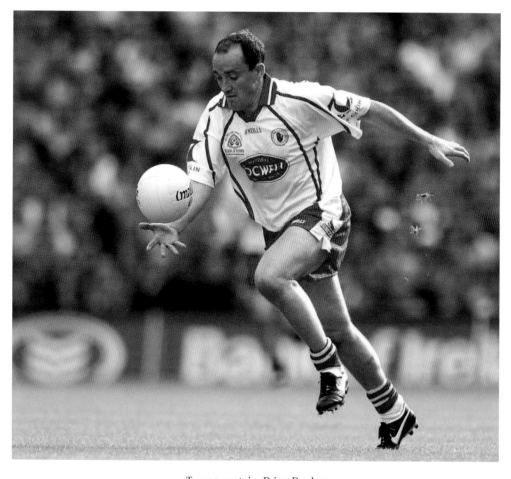

Tyrone captain, Brian Dooher

2005 ALL-IRELAND
SENIOR FOOTBALL CHAMPIONSHIP FINAL

SCORERS – TYRONE: Owen Mulligan 0-4; Stephen O'Neill 0-4; Peter Canavan 1-1; Brian McGuigan 0-3; Ryan Mellon 0-2; Brian Dooher 0-1; Philip Jordan 0-1

SCORERS – KERRY: Colm Cooper 0-5; Dara Ó Cinnéide 1-1; Tomás Ó Sé 1-0; Darragh Ó Sé 0-2; Eoin Brosnan 0-2

TYRONE

Pascal McConnell

Michael McGee   Joe McMahon   Ryan McMenamin

Davy Harte   Conor Gormley   Philip Jordan

Enda McGinley   Seán Cavanagh

Brian Dooher *(Captain)*   Brian McGuigan   Ryan Mellon

Peter Canavan   Stephen O'Neill   Owen Mulligan

SUBSTITUTES: Colin Holmes for Peter Canavan; Chris Lawn for Joe McMahon; Peter Canavan for Enda McGinley

KERRY

Diarmuid Murphy

Mike McCarthy   Aidan O'Mahony   Tom O'Sullivan

Tomás Ó Sé   Marc Ó Sé   Séamus Moynihan

Darragh Ó Sé   William Kirby

Liam Hassett   Eoin Brosnan   Paul Galvin

Colm Cooper   Declan O'Sullivan *(Captain)*   Dara Ó Cinnéide

SUBSTITUTES: Mike Frank Russell for Liam Hassett;
Darran O'Sullivan for Dara Ó Cinnéide;
Eamonn Fitzmaurice for Séamus Moynihan;
Bryan Sheehan for Paul Galvin

TYRONE – 2005

Back row, left to right: Conor Gormley, Ciarán Gourley, Eoin Bradley, Ryan McMenamin, Peter Donnelly, Colin Holmes, Joe McMahon, Stephen O'Neill, Seán Cavanagh, Pascal McConnell, Owen Mulligan, John Devine, Gavin Devlin, Shane Sweeney, Michael Murphy, Brian Meenan
Front row, left to right: Mark Harte, Brendan Donnelly, Chris Lawn, Ryan Mellon, Davy Harte, Enda McGinley, Martin Penrose, Brian Dooher, Philip Jordan, Brian McGuigan, Michael McGee, Peter Canavan, Colm McCullagh, Leo Meenan

Tyrone manager, Mickey Harte

2005 ALL-STARS FOOTBALL SELECTION

Diarmuid Murphy
(Kerry) 2nd

Ryan McMenamin
(Tyrone) 1st

Mike McCarthy
(Kerry) 3rd

Andy Mallon
(Armagh) 1st

Tomás Ó Sé
(Kerry) 2nd

Conor Gormley
(Tyrone) 2nd

Philip Jordan
(Tyrone) 2nd

Seán Cavanagh
(Tyrone) 3rd

Paul McGrane
(Armagh) 2nd

Brian Dooher
(Tyrone) 2nd

Peter Canavan
(Tyrone) 6th

Owen Mulligan
(Tyrone) 1st

Colm Cooper
(Kerry) 3rd

Stephen O'Neill
(Tyrone) 2nd

Steven McDonnell
(Armagh) 3rd

2006
ALL-IRELAND
FOOTBALL FINAL

SUNDAY, SEPTEMBER 17

KERRY VERSUS MAYO

CROKE PARK

REFEREE: BRIAN CROWE
(CAVAN)

KERRY 4-15 MAYO 3-5

One player more than any other defined the 2006 Senior Football Championship, which culminated with market leaders Kerry winning their 34th title with a comprehensive 13-point defeat of a Mayo team that experienced yet another nightmare on Final Sunday at Croke Park.

Kieran Donaghy lined out at midfield in three of Kerry's four games in Munster, including the drawn final against Cork, but he missed the Kingdom's defeat in the provincial final replay because of suspension.

Manager Jack O'Connor selected Donaghy at full-forward against Longford in the round four qualifier and the Austin Stacks clubman proceeded to change the course of the season.

Yes, Donaghy's influence was indeed that significant.

Consider this: Kerry played four games in the Munster Championship - against Waterford, Tipperary and Cork (twice) - and failed to score a goal.

But in four subsequent matches at the business end of the campaign - against Longford, Armagh, Cork and Mayo - Jack O'Connor's reshaped side scored no fewer than 11 goals.

Donaghy's capacity to win high ball and lay it off to well-placed team-mates proved a crucial component in Kerry's rejuvenated attack.

Donaghy also displayed his own net-finding ability when he fielded a high ball from Tommy Griffin in the All-Ireland final against Mayo and got past David Heaney to finish superbly.

That goal by Donaghy came in the 8th minute but was actually Kerry's second goal - Declan O'Sullivan had put the ball in the Mayo net just 60 seconds earlier.

And Colm Cooper's goal in the 26th minute left Kerry 3-6 to 1-0 ahead.

The impressive Kevin O'Neill scored that Mayo goal in the 16th minute.

Indeed the Connacht champions struck for two further goals just before half-time, from midfielder Pat Harte and the ever-dangerous O'Neill; yet Kerry still led at the break by six points, 3-8 to 3-2.

KERRY - 2006

Back row, left to right: Daniel Bohan, Ronan Hussey, Eoin Brosnan, Darragh Ó Sé, Bryan Sheehan, Mike McCarthy, Marc Ó Sé, Aodán Mac Gearailt, Diarmuid Murphy, Tom O'Sullivan, Paul Galvin, Kieran Donaghy, Killian Young, Ronan O'Connor, Brendan Guiney
Front row, left to right: Paul O'Connor, Darran O'Sullivan, Mossie Lyons, Eamonn Fitzmaurice, Seán O'Sullivan, Séamus Moynihan, Tommy Griffin, Declan O'Sullivan, Aidan O'Mahony, Tomás Ó Sé, Colm Cooper, Mike Frank Russell, Pádraig Reidy, Kieran Cremin, Adrian O'Connell, Kieran O'Leary

Kerry manager, Jack O'Connor

2006 ALL-STARS FOOTBALL SELECTION

Stephen Cluxton
(Dublin) 2nd

Marc Ó Sé
(Kerry) 1st

Barry Owens
(Fermanagh) 2nd

Karl Lacey
(Donegal) 1st

Séamus Moynihan
(Kerry) 3rd

Ger Spillane
(Cork) 1st

Aidan O'Mahony
(Kerry) 1st

Darragh Ó Sé
(Kerry) 3rd

Nicholas Murphy
(Cork) 1st

Paul Galvin
(Kerry) 2nd

Alan Brogan
(Dublin) 1st

Alan Dillon
(Mayo) 1st

Conor Mortimer
(Mayo) 1st

Kieran Donaghy
(Kerry) 1st

Ronan Clarke
(Armagh) 1st

2007
ALL-IRELAND
FOOTBALL FINAL

SUNDAY, SEPTEMBER 16

KERRY VERSUS CORK

CROKE PARK

REFEREE: DAVID COLDRICK
(MEATH)

KERRY 3-13 CORK 1-9

Kerry became the first county since 1990 to retain the title following a 10-point victory over Cork in what was a first-ever all-Munster, All-Ireland final.

Clearly the pressure was on the Kerry players in advance of the final, all the more so, given that Cork supporters let it be known that a victory for their team would wipe away all the heartbreak and disappointment endured at the hands of their arch-rivals down through the decades.

The stakes were high and, ultimately, the manner of Kerry's victory was especially noteworthy.

Kieran Donaghy scored two goals while Colm Cooper produced a superb display and finished with a tally of 1-5 as well as the 'Man of the Match' award.

Cooper scored the first goal of the game in the 17th minute when he flicked the ball to the net despite the presence of his marker Kieran O'Connor and the Cork goalkeeper Alan Quirke, who came off his line to contest a high ball from Séamus Scanlon.

Kerry mostly played two forwards – Cooper and Donaghy – up front which resulted in a very packed middle-third area.

Kerry held a 1-6 to 0-6 advantage at the end of a ragged and free-ridden opening half.

Donaghy had claims for a penalty turned down when he appeared to be fouled by Michael Shields in the 23rd minute but nothing accrued.

Michael Cussen kicked an excellent point from play in the first half, while Cork's other scores came from frees – three from James Masters and two from the energetic Donncha O'Connor.

Cooper scored 1-2 in that opening period for Kerry while his team-mates Aidan O'Mahony, Paul Galvin and Tomás Ó Se contributed a point each from play and Bryan Sheehan converted a free.

Cork's challenge evaporated once Donaghy scored his first goal 26 seconds after the re-start which pushed Kerry six points clear.

Ironically, Cork had conceded just one goal on their way to the final and their reputation was built on a strong defensive formation which largely failed to function in the final.

Kerry responded to the challenge in style and dictated the play in the second half against a strangely subdued Cork team forced to line out without the injured Anthony Lynch, who replaced John Miskella early in the second half.

But there was little a brave Lynch - who broke a bone in his hand in a practice match on the Saturday week before the final, or a struggling Cork team could do at that stage to stem the tide.

James Masters, who had missed the semi-final win over Meath because of a broken jaw sustained against Sligo in the quarter-final, bravely played from the start and even though he scored three points from frees, the Nemo Rangers marksman was clearly not as effective as usual and was replaced by Daniel Goulding at half-time.

Goulding scored 1-1 and was one of the few Cork players to make a meaningful impact against a rampant Kerry side.

Goulding's goal in the 53rd minute – a low hard shot to the corner of the net – was brilliantly taken and gave Cork some impetus.

Noel O'Leary and Shields were Cork's most industrious defenders on a day when too many of their team-mates performed below par.

Darragh Ó Se played a key role in Kerry's success with a fine display against Cork midfielder Nicholas Murphy, who had been the form player coming into the final.

Ó Sé and his excellent midfield partner, Séamus Scanlon raised the standard and had a distinct advantage in the middle of the park, which ensured that Kerry prospered.

Kerry's experience on big-match day was a telling factor, whereas Cork lost their way once Donaghy kicked the ball into an empty net.

Quirke had moved out to the left of his goal in anticipation of a pass from Ger Spillane, but Donaghy dispossessed the Ballygarvan man and the big Kerry full-forward was as surprised as everyone else to see a wide-open goal.

It was soul-destroying for Cork.

Donaghy struck for his second goal 14 minutes after the restart when, despite the attention of Quirke and Shields, the Austin Stacks man knocked down a high ball from Eoin Brosnan before finishing to the net in style.

It was another defensive error but Donaghy has to be given full credit for exacting the maximum punishment on Cork.

Cork's short-passing game came unstuck in the face of ferocious pressure from a highly-motivated Kerry side with an insatiable appetite for hard work.

Tomás Ó Sé, Galvin and O'Mahony won a huge amount of breaking ball and used it intelligently.

Cussen looked threatening for Cork whenever high ball was sent into the full-forward line but his team-mates seldom resorted to the long ball, persisting instead with the short game, which played into Kerry's hands.

Cork gave away hard-won possession cheaply and Kerry took full advantage.

Apart from the chief scorers, Cooper and Donaghy, no fewer than seven other Kerry players found the target in what overall was a magnificent team performance by Kerry.

Kerry captain, Declan O'Sullivan

SCORERS – KERRY: Colm Cooper 1-5; Kieran Donaghy 2-0; Bryan Sheehan 0-2; Paul Galvin 0-1; Seán O'Sullivan 0-1; Tomás Ó Sé 0-1; Aidan O'Mahony 0-1; Séamus Scanlon 0-1; Declan O'Sullivan 0-1

SCORERS – CORK: Donncha O'Connor 0-4; Daniel Goulding 1-1; James Masters 0-3; Michael Cussen 0-1

KERRY

Diarmuid Murphy

Marc Ó Sé   Tom O'Sullivan   Pádraig Reidy

Aidan O'Mahony   Tomás Ó Sé   Killian Young

Darragh Ó Sé   Séamus Scanlon

Paul Galvin   Declan O'Sullivan *(Captain)*   Eoin Brosnan

Colm Cooper   Kieran Donaghy   Bryan Sheehan

SUBSTITUTES: Seán O'Sullivan for Paul Galvin; Darran O'Sullivan for Eoin Brosnan; Tommy Griffin for Killian Young; Mike Frank Russell for Bryan Sheehan; Mossie Lyons for Pádraig Reidy

CORK

Alan Quirke

Michael Shields   Graham Canty   Kieran O'Connor

Noel O'Leary   Ger Spillane   John Miskella

Derek Kavanagh *(Captain)*   Nicholas Murphy

Conor McCarthy   Pearse O'Neill   Kevin McMahon

James Masters   Michael Cussen   Donncha O'Connor

SUBSTITUTES: Daniel Goulding for James Masters; Anthony Lynch for John Miskella; Fintan Goold for Kevin McMahon; Kevin O'Sullivan for Conor McCarthy

KERRY - 2007

Back row, left to right: Daniel Bohan, Tommy Walsh, Ronan Hussey, Darragh Ó Sé, Paul Galvin, Kieran Donaghy, Marc Ó Sé, Tom O'Sullivan, Diarmuid Murphy, Séamus Scanlon, Killian Young, Mike Quirke, Declan Quill, Donnchadh Walsh, Ronán Ó Flatharta
Front row, left to right: Mike Frank Russell, Mossie Lyons, Paul O'Connor, Darran O'Sullivan, Seán O'Sullivan, Eoin Brosnan, Pádraig Reidy, Bryan Sheehan, Declan O'Sullivan, Aidan O'Mahony, Tomás Ó Sé, Colm Cooper, Tommy Griffin, Kieran O'Leary, Kieran Cremin

Kerry manager, Pat O'Shea

2007 ALL-STARS FOOTBALL SELECTION

Stephen Cluxton
(Dublin) 3rd

Marc Ó Sé
(Kerry) 2nd

Kevin McCloy
(Derry) 1st

Graham Canty
(Cork) 1st

Tomás Ó Sé
(Kerry) 3rd

Aidan O'Mahony
(Kerry) 2nd

Barry Cahill
(Dublin) 1st

Ciarán Whelan
(Dublin) 2nd

Darragh Ó Sé
(Kerry) 4th

Stephen Bray
(Meath) 1st

Declan O'Sullivan
(Kerry) 1st

Alan Brogan
(Dublin) 2nd

Colm Cooper
(Kerry) 4th

Paddy Bradley
(Derry) 1st

Tommy Freeman
(Monaghan) 1st

2008
ALL–IRELAND
FOOTBALL FINAL

SUNDAY, SEPTEMBER 21

TYRONE VERSUS KERRY

CROKE PARK

**REFEREE: MAURICE DEEGAN
(LAOIS)**

TYRONE 1-15 KERRY 0-14

The talk all year was of Kerry's pursuit of the three-in-a-row but it failed to materialise and instead it was Mickey Harte's Tyrone who captured their third All-Ireland title this decade.

Tyrone came out on top in the three championship clashes between the counties; the 2003 semi-final and the finals of 2005 and 2008.

It was extra special for Tyrone for several reasons.

Harte had been criticised in some quarters in his own county following his team's defeat by Down in the Ulster Championship but the inspirational manager never doubted his own or his players' ability to fight back against the odds.

It was Tyrone's first championship clash with Kerry since Kieran Donaghy emerged on the scene and Harte's tactics proved extremely successful in limiting the threat of the Austin Stacks clubman.

Moreover, when Tyrone defeated Kerry in the 2005 showpiece, the side featured the brilliant Brian McGuigan at centre-half-forward and the lethal full-forward line of Peter Canavan, Stephen O'Neill and Owen Mulligan.

None of those four started against Kerry this time; Canavan had retired while O'Neill, Mulligan and McGuigan came on as substitutes to illustrate just how the team had evolved.

In fact, astonishingly, in the space of five years, there were no fewer than 9 changes in the Tyrone starting 15 against Armagh in 2003 from the side that lined out against Kerry in the 2008 Final.

Tyrone had due respect for Kerry but clearly had no fear whatsoever of the kingpins of Gaelic Football as evidenced once again in the 2008 final.

Harte proved his pedigree as an outstanding manager and master tactician and his decision to switch Joe McMahon from attack to defence at the start was highly effective in curbing the twin threat of Donaghy and Tommy Walsh.

Kerry were simply unable to reap the benefit of the long-ball tactic because of the physical presence of the McMahon brothers and Conor Gormley while half-backs Davy

Harte, Philip Jordan and Ryan McMenamin defended tenaciously and then counter-attacked with menace.

There was one enforced change on the Tyrone team with Pascal McConnell taking over in goal from John Devine, who had to withdraw from the team following the sad death of his father on the eve of the final.

McConnell was quite magnificent and denied Kerry a certain two goals – firstly blocking a rasping shot from Tommy Walsh in the 22nd minute and then somehow keeping out a goalbound shot from Declan O'Sullivan in the closing minutes at the expense of a '45.

Bryan Sheehan kicked wide from that '45 before being replaced by David Moran.

Had O'Sullivan found the net at that vital juncture with Tyrone just one point ahead, Kerry might well have won their 36th title.

As it was, Tyrone drove on relentlessly and were rewarded with points from the towering midfielder Enda McGinley and substitutes Kevin Hughes and Colm Cavanagh.

Hughes, despite hitting three wides, made a big impact when introduced for Colin Holmes at half-time in a game of fierce intensity.

The sides were level on no fewer than seven occasions in the opening half and twice more after the break to emphasise the close and competitive nature of the match.

Colm Cooper scored four points - one from play – which ensured that Kerry held a slender 0-8 to 0-7 half-time advantage.

Kerry played defensively and, consequently, were unable to deliver enough quality ball into Donaghy, Walsh and the in-form Cooper, who troubled Conor Gormley on occasions.

But Kerry's inability to utilise Cooper to his maximum, due to Tyrone's tactical astuteness, proved costly and Gormley grew in confidence as the game progressed.

Harte, Jordan and McMenamin continued to push forward while, in marked contrast, Bryan Sheehan and Eoin Brosnan found it difficult to make much progress.

The impressive Davy Harte scored a superb point from play in that first half while Dooher withstood three hefty tackles to land a truly spectacular point following a powerful run.

Another notable feature of the first half was Declan O'Sullivan's block on Seán Cavanagh as the Tyrone full-forward kicked for a point.

But overall, it proved a near impossible task for the Kerry defence to curtail the influence of Cavanagh, who produced a superb display and finished with a tally of five points from play.

Kevin Hughes won the breaking ball at the re-start and surged forward before kicking the ball into Stephen O'Neill, who had replaced the injured Colm McCullagh in the 21st minute.

O'Neill, who had come out of retirement just eighteen days earlier, did exceptionally well to play the ball into the onrushing Hughes, whose shot was half-blocked before it was kicked to the net by Tommy McGuigan.

O'Neill more than justified his return with that sublime pass for the goal that ultimately left Kerry chasing the game.

Ryan Mellon then pointed as Tyrone increased their lead to three points.

But Kerry still had plenty to offer as Pat O'Shea's side outscored Tyrone 0-6 to 0-2 from the 43rd to the 57th minute.

Dooher and Cavanagh found the range for Tyrone during that period while Cooper scored two points for Kerry with a point each coming from lively substitute Darran O'Sullivan, Tommy Walsh, Tomás Ó Sé and Darragh Ó Sé.

But with the game at a critical stage, it was the highly influential Cavanagh who took the challenge to mighty Kerry, winning hard ball and scoring two excellent points from play.

By now Paul Galvin had replaced Tommy Walsh on a faltering Kerry team.

Pascal McConnell then produced a wonder save to deny Declan O'Sullivan a goal and thereafter Tyrone took control.

Enda McGinley, Hughes and Colm Cavanagh landed a point apiece as Tyrone closed out the game to make their own history and in the process deny Kerry the three-in-a-row.

SCORERS – TYRONE: Seán Cavanagh 0-5; Tommy McGuigan 1-1;
Brian Dooher 0-2; Davy Harte 0-1; Colm McCullagh 0-1;
Martin Penrose 0-1; Ryan Mellon 0-1;
Colm Cavanagh 0-1; Enda McGinley 0-1; Kevin Hughes 0-1

SCORERS – KERRY: Colm Cooper 0-6; Bryan Sheehan 0-2; Declan O'Sullivan 0-2;
Darran O'Sullivan 0-1; Tommy Walsh 0-1; Tomás Ó Sé 0-1;
Darragh Ó Sé 0-1

TYRONE

Pascal McConnell

Joe McMahon   Justin McMahon   Conor Gormley

Davy Harte   Philip Jordan   Ryan McMenamin

Colin Holmes   Enda McGinley

Brian Dooher *(Captain)*   Martin Penrose   Ryan Mellon

Tommy McGuigan   Seán Cavanagh   Colm McCullagh

SUBSTITUTES: Stephen O'Neill for Colm McCullagh; Kevin Hughes for Colin Holmes;
Brian McGuigan for Martin Penrose; Owen Mulligan for Ryan Mellon;
Colm Cavanagh for Tommy McGuigan

KERRY

Diarmuid Murphy

Marc Ó Sé   Tom O'Sullivan   Pádraig Reidy

Tomás Ó Sé *(Captain)*   Aidan O'Mahony   Killian Young

Darragh Ó Sé   Séamus Scanlon

Eoin Brosnan   Declan O'Sullivan   Bryan Sheehan

Colm Cooper   Kieran Donaghy   Tommy Walsh

SUBSTITUTES: Darran O'Sullivan for Eoin Brosnan;
Tommy Griffin for Séamus Scanlon;
Paul Galvin for Tommy Walsh; David Moran for Bryan Sheehan

TYRONE – 2008

Back row, left to right: Raymond Mulgrew, Damien McCaul, Justin McMahon, Colm Cavanagh, Owen Mulligan, Jonathan Curran, Seán Cavanagh, Pascal McConnell, Colin Holmes, Shaun O'Neill, Cathal McCarron, Peter Donnelly, Paul Quinn, Kevin Hughes, Brian McGuigan, Stephen O'Neill
Middle row: Conor Gormley, Joe McMahon, Niall Gormley, Davy Harte, Tommy McGuigan, Enda McGinley, Philip Jordan, Brian Dooher, Ryan Mellon, Martin Penrose, Colm McCullagh, Michael McGee, Ciarán Gourley
Front row: P.J. Quinn, Ryan McMenamin, Dermot Carlin

Tyrone manager, Mickey Harte

2008 ALL-STARS FOOTBALL SELECTION

Gary Connaughton
(Westmeath) 1st

Conor Gormley
(Tyrone) 3rd

Justin McMahon
(Tyrone) 1st

John Keane
(Westmeath) 2nd

Davy Harte
(Tyrone) 1st

Tomás Ó Sé
(Kerry) 4th

Philip Jordan
(Tyrone) 3rd

Enda McGinley
(Tyrone) 1st

Shane Ryan
(Dublin) 1st

Brian Dooher
(Tyrone) 3rd

Declan O'Sullivan
(Kerry) 2nd

Seán Cavanagh
(Tyrone) 4th

Colm Cooper
(Kerry) 5th

Kieran Donaghy
(Kerry) 2nd

Ronan Clarke
(Armagh) 2nd

2009
ALL-IRELAND
FOOTBALL FINAL

SUNDAY, SEPTEMBER 20

KERRY VERSUS CORK

CROKE PARK

REFEREE: MARTY DUFFY
(SLIGO)

KERRY 0-16 CORK 1-9

Bertrand Russell once wrote that 'to be without some of the things you want is an indispensable part of happiness'.

I can only assume that Bertrand never met a player who suffered the awful pain of losing in an All-Ireland football or hurling final.

Cork captain Graham Canty and his team-mates were all shattered when Sligo referee Marty Duffy blew the whistle to signal the end of the 2009 All-Ireland football final.

Typically, Kerry displayed all their craft, experience and mental strength to overcome their arch-rivals by four points and in doing so claimed their 36th All-Ireland title.

Cork came to Croke Park on a mission and the Rebels' form in 'Championship 2009' suggested that the 19-year wait for the Sam Maguire Cup would come to an end.

After all, Cork had comfortably disposed of Kerry by eight points in the replayed Munster semi-final and there was a sense that Conor Counihan's side had learned from past defeats on the big stage in Croke Park and that their day of destiny had arrived.

Almost all those who predicted a Cork win, especially after their impressive display against Tyrone in the semi-final, stressed the importance of not allowing Kerry take a grip of the game in the opening quarter.

As it transpired, Cork dictated the early pace and Colm O'Neill scored a superb goal just past the 10 minute mark to leave his side 1-3 to 0-1 ahead.

Kerry full-back Tommy Griffin slipped as O'Neill raced on to a free kick from Nicholas Murphy and then beat Kerry goalkeeper Diarmuid Murphy at the near post.

The Ballyclough clubman finished to the roof of the net with power and aplomb.

But Griffin, who struggled early on, recovered his composure and went on to play a significant role in Kerry's victory.

It was a mark of Griffin's mental strength as much as his honest footballing ability that he eventually came out on top against O'Neill.

Strangely, the game changed in favour of Kerry following the Cork goal.

Séamus Scanlon began to exert his influence at midfield and the under-pressure Cork backs were forced to concede frees which were converted by Colm Cooper.

Tommy Walsh scored two excellent points from play which brought Kerry back into the game with a vengeance.

Then Declan O'Sullivan proceeded to land a splendid point in the 28th minute to level the match for the second time.

Former Aussie Rules player Tadhg Kennelly kicked over his second point to put Kerry 0-9 to 1-4 ahead but Daniel Goulding replied with a point for Cork.

Kennelly had a fine game and had the measure of Graham Canty until he was surprisingly substituted midway through the second half.

Kennelly was into the thick of the action right from the start.

He raced out from his half forward position at the throw-in and, as Nicholas Murphy won the ball, the Listowel Emmets man came in on the blind side and caught the Cork midfielder on the chin.

Kennelly later said that he intended to make an immediate impact but did not and would not intentionally go out to hurt another footballer.

Kennelly gave up a professional contract in Aussie Rules to follow his childhood dream and win an All-Ireland medal like his brother Noel and their late-lamented father Tim, who captained Kerry to All-Ireland success in 1979.

Kerry dominated the second quarter and had moved 0-11 to 1-6 ahead at half-time.

Kerry's second score after the break should have been disallowed as team captain Darran O'Sullivan bounced the ball twice before kicking a point.

O'Sullivan worked extremely hard and had a fine game before being replaced by Kieran Donaghy in the 57th minute.

But in the cut and thrust of an All-Ireland final, little things can make a huge difference and, quite frankly, Cork squandered too many chances early in the second half when in control.

Cork gave away hard-won possession far too cheaply and their play suffered through indecisiveness.

Furthermore, Cork shot no fewer than 14 wides in the course of the match, including 10 in the second half.

Kerry's wide tally amounted to six.

Still, Cork had reduced the deficit to a single point when Daniel Goulding converted a free with 15 minutes remaining.

Donncha O'Connor had a gilt-edged opportunity to level the match but his attempted point effort was brilliantly blocked by Marc Ó Sé and the ball was moved upfield where Tommy Walsh scored a point following a fine passage of play from Kerry.

Walsh then landed his fourth point from play and Tomás Ó Sé rowed in with his second point to extend Kerry's advantage to four points.

O'Connor was one of Cork's genuine scoring threats during the summer and he had a real battle against the impressive Marc Ó Sé in the final itself.

Apart from the early lapse, the Kerry defence was superb, none more so than Tom O'Sullivan, who produced an outstanding display while Mike McCarthy was never less than assured and confident at centre half back and won his personal duel with Pearse O'Neill.

McCarthy, who retired following Kerry's All-Ireland victory in 2006, had a fine season after returning to the inter-county scene for the qualifier match against Sligo.

His displays in the latter stages of the Championship make a mockery of all the months of hard slog and training that many inter-county panels have to undertake as managers push out the boundary.

On the evidence of McCarthy's form after such a long lay-off, it proved once again the futility of all the heavy training that inter-county panels engage in year after year.

Players can run all day long and spend night after night in gyms but nothing compares to practicing the skills.

Galvin, Declan O'Sullivan, Kennelly, Tomás Ó Sé and Scanlon led the way for Kerry in winning the breaking ball and forcing the pace at every opportunity.

Kerry defended en-masse in the closing ten minutes with often up to a dozen players behind the ball and Cork never appeared likely to get through for much-needed scores.

Goulding created a goal chance in the 48th minute for Cork but his shot was blocked by the very alert Kerry goalkeeper, Diarmuid Murphy.

There was a marked absence in Cork's play of the power and pace that was so evident in the semi-final against Tyrone.

The old failings came back to haunt the Cork players and Kerry, never a team to need an invitation, took full advantage of any shortcomings.

Apart from their wastefulness in front of the posts, Cork's handling of the ball also let them down on occasions.

Galvin and Tomás Ó Sé were prominent in taking advantage of Cork's errors.

Kerry adhered to their game plan and never once panicked whereas Cork, despite the dream start, found it difficult to play with the fluency that was the hallmark of their early season form.

The fact that Graham Canty and Pearse O'Neill were unable to make the significant contributions of earlier matches also impacted on Cork's overall play.

Kerry manager Jack O'Connor made some necessary changes as the Championship unfolded.

Griffin was a success when moved to the troublesome full back position; McCarthy brought a new-found confidence to centre-half-back while Scanlon proved highly effective at midfield.

But clearly the return of McCarthy was a major factor why Kerry turned their season around and regained the title.

Jack O'Connor convinced the Kilcummin man to return to inter-county football promising him a more creative role in the half back line and the brave gamble paid off for both player and manager.

There was talk of trouble in the Kerry camp during the summer and their play in the early rounds suggested all was not right in the kingdom of football.

Colm Cooper and Tomás Ó Sé were left on the bench for the game against Antrim after a breach of discipline but both players were called into the fray before match end as Kerry struggled against the beaten Ulster finalists.

However, Cooper and Ó Sé accepted their punishment and both players made a significant contribution towards Kerry's memorable and hugely successful season.

Jack O'Connor, Cooper, Ó Sé plus the rest of the Kerry panel and backroom team moved on and it was all back slapping and friendly greetings once the Sam Maguire Cup was secured for another year.

Paul Galvin, who missed most of the 2008 Championship campaign through suspension, put the disappointment of his sending off against Cork in the Munster semi-final replay behind him, to emerge as one of Kerry's most influential players in Championship 2009.

Indeed, the Finuge man made such an important contribution to Kerry's season that he held off strong opposition from his teammate Tomás Ó Sé and Cork captain Graham Canty to win the GAA 'Footballer of the Year Award'.

It was a long and difficult season for Kerry but it culminated with one of the most satisfying victories for this present generation of footballers in the 125th Anniversary of the G.A.A.

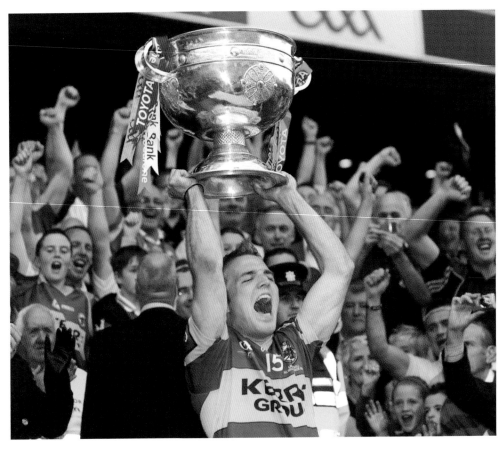

Kerry captain, Darran O'Sullivan

SCORERS – KERRY: Colm Cooper 0-6; Tommy Walsh 0-4; Tadhg Kennelly 0-2; Tomás Ó Sé 0-2; Declan O'Sullivan 0-1; Darran O'Sullivan 0-1

SCORERS – CORK: Daniel Goulding 0-4; Colm O'Neill 1-1; Donncha O'Connor 0-3; Patrick Kelly 0-1

KERRY

Diarmuid Murphy

Marc Ó Sé	Tommy Griffin	Tom O'Sullivan
Tomás Ó Sé	Mike McCarthy	Killian Young

Darragh Ó Sé   Séamus Scanlon

Darran O'Sullivan *(Captain)*	Tadhg Kennelly	Paul Galvin
Colm Cooper	Declan O'Sullivan	Tommy Walsh

SUBSTITUTES: Donnchadh Walsh for Tadhg Kennelly; Mike Quirke for Darragh Ó Sé; Kieran Donaghy for Darran O'Sullivan; David Moran for Tommy Walsh; Aidan O'Mahony for Killian Young

CORK

Alan Quirke

Michael Shields	Kieran O'Connor	Anthony Lynch
Noel O'Leary	Graham Canty *(Captain)*	John Miskella

Alan O'Connor   Nicholas Murphy

Patrick Kelly	Pearse O'Neill	Paul Kerrigan
Daniel Goulding	Colm O'Neill	Donncha O'Connor

SUBSTITUTES: Eoin Cadogan for Kieran O'Connor; Fintan Goold for Paul Kerrigan; Derek Kavanagh for Anthony Lynch; James Masters for Daniel Goulding; Michael Cussen for Alan O'Connor

Back row, left to right: Tadhg Kennelly, Ger Reidy, Daniel Bohan, Darragh O'Shea, Bryan Sheehan, Paul Galvin, Aidan O'Mahony, Tom O'Sullivan, Marc Ó Sé, Seán O'Sullivan, Diarmuid Murphy, Séamus Scanlon, Aidan O'Shea, Donnchadh Walsh, Tommy Walsh, Mike Quirke, Maurice Corridan, Kieran Donaghy, Anthony Maher, David Moran, Ronán Ó Flatharta, Kieran Quirke
Front row, left to right: Paul O'Connor, Mike McCarthy, Declan O'Sullivan, Killian Young, Darran O'Sullivan, Tomas Ó Sé, Tommy Griffin, Colm Cooper, Pádraig Reidy, Barry John Walsh

Kerry manager, Jack O'Connor

2009 ALL-STARS FOOTBALL SELECTION

Diarmuid Murphy
(Kerry) 3rd

Karl Lacey
(Donegal) 2nd

Michael Shields
(Cork) 1st

Tom O'Sullivan
(Kerry) 2nd

Tomás Ó Sé
(Kerry) 5th

Graham Canty
(Cork) 2nd

John Miskella
(Cork) 1st

Dermot Earley
(Kildare) 2nd

Séamus Scanlon
(Kerry) 1st

Paul Galvin
(Kerry) 3rd

Pearse O'Neill
(Cork) 1st

Tadhg Kennelly
(Kerry) 1st

Daniel Goulding
(Cork) 1st

Declan O'Sullivan
(Kerry) 3rd

Stephen O'Neill
(Tyrone) 3rd

2010
ALL-IRELAND
FOOTBALL FINAL

SUNDAY, SEPTEMBER 19

CORK VERSUS DOWN

CROKE PARK

REFEREE: DAVID COLDRICK
(MEATH)

CORK 0-16 DOWN 0-15

It was a long and sometimes arduous journey for Cork's footballers but the hard work eventually paid off and their mighty captain, Graham Canty from Bantry Blues, had the proud honour of accepting the Sam Maguire Cup from fellow Corkonian, GAA president Christy Cooney.

Canty, who had struggled with a hamstring injury before the final against Down, made a significant impact after coming on as a substitute early in the second half.

Nicholas Murphy also made a valuable contribution as a substitute while both Daniel Goulding and Donncha O'Connor were hugely impressive in the forward division.

Goulding scored nine points, including two from play and three '45s, while O'Connor landed five points, most notably three from open play.

Eoin Cadogan, Michael Shields and Aidan Walsh were highly effective throughout and were among Cork's more accomplished players, even at times when the Rebels' play lacked cohesion.

Goalkeeper Alan Quirke was composed and confident for Cork and was always in control with his handling, passing and kick-outs.

Daniel Hughes and Paul McComiskey scored three points each from play for Down and always posed a serious threat in attack.

Given his impressive display, it was surprising that McComiskey was substituted in the 56th minute as he looked well capable of notching further scores.

Down goalkeeper Brendan McVeigh made two fine saves from Ciarán Sheehan and Colm O'Neill, and all round produced an excellent display of goalkeeping.

There was nothing straightforward about Cork's seventh All-Ireland title and first in 20 years, as it necessitated playing 8 games, highlighted by a one-point victory in the final itself.

The relief among all the players and team manager Conor Counihan was plain for all to see when referee David Coldrick called a halt to proceedings on Final Sunday.

Cork had survived, if only just, and Counihan joined an illustrious group who have achieved All-Ireland senior successes as a manager and a player.

Counihan was a central part of the Cork team that won All-Ireland titles in 1989 and 1990 and, as manager, was the driving force behind the 2010 success.

He never stopped believing, despite numerous setbacks, that his Cork team had the ability to win ultimate honours and defy the critics.

Cork players proved, once and for all, that they had the courage and skill to deliver when the stakes were highest.

Ultimately, it was Cork's craft and experience that saw them emerge from some difficult stages against a determined and skilful Down team that showed no discernible trace of big-match nerves.

Down goalkeeper Brendan McVeigh denied Ciarán Sheehan a goal with a fine block in the first minute as Cork started at a blistering pace.

Sheehan fisted the rebound but Daniel McCartan prevented the ball from going over the line.

Cork's inability to put away those early chances appeared to affect their confidence and Down began to dictate the play as James McCartan's side moved 0-7 to 0-2 ahead by the 27th minute.

McComiskey, Hughes and Marty Clarke scored two points apiece for Down during that dominant phase while John Clarke tacked on a point.

Clearly, Cork were in trouble at that juncture and in serious danger of losing their shape.

The fact that Cork survived that rocky period clearly underlined the character and mental strength of the players.

There was no panic.

Cork had something to prove and were in no mood to take a backward step.

Losing to Kerry in both the 2007 and 2009 All-Ireland finals had steeled the resolve of this group of Cork players, who were determined to stand firm against a confident Down side.

Noel O'Leary was deployed to man-mark Down playmaker Marty Clarke and the Cill na Martra clubman largely limited the influence of the former Aussie Rules player.

Still Clarke created some openings with neat passes and also hit over three points from frees.

But O'Leary never relented and Clarke found it difficult to get on the ball and failed to score from play.

Goulding scored Cork's first point from play in the 32nd minute and O'Connor added another from play before half-time, at the end of which Down held an 0-8 to 0-5 advantage.

Cork had won an abundance of possession in that opening half but their play was ragged and the players looked anything but confident.

In fact, Cork were somewhat fortunate not to be further in arrears.

Down utilised the long diagonal ball to good effect while Cork struggled to make progress through the centre.

Murphy came on for Cork at the start of the second half and made an immediate impact.

Canty joined the fray shortly afterwards and his presence, coupled with that of Murphy's, proved hugely beneficial for Cork.

Walsh's high fielding under pressure was a feature of the match and the young Kanturk man left an indelible imprint in his first appearance in an All-Ireland senior final.

Patrick Kelly was hard working and creative while Colm O'Neill proved influential when introduced in the final quarter and his pace and skill troubled the Down backs.

Paul Kerrigan continually ran at the Down defence and also kicked a valuable point from play.

However, Cork were still chasing the game when Mark Poland fired over a point from play to leave Down 0-10 to 0-7 ahead by the 45th minute.

The Ulster side had no intention of wilting under pressure although Murphy and Walsh were strong in midfield for Cork and continued to win clean possession.

Slowly but surely the tide turned.

Down clearly missed the influence of their injured midfielder and team captain Ambrose Rogers whereas Cork had several big names on the bench to call on.

Cork began to adopt a more direct approach and the inside forward line benefited immensely from quick early ball.

O'Connor, Goulding and Sheehan sent over a point each from play to level the match with 20 minutes still remaining.

Predictably, Cork players grew in confidence following that scoring flurry.

Kevin McKernan edged Down ahead again with a fine point from play following good work from Mark Poland but Cork hit back as the strong-running Kerrigan found the target and the outstanding Goulding scored from two high-pressure '45s.

In the closing minutes, Peter Fitzpatrick landed a point from play for a spirited Down side.

O'Connor and Ronan Murtagh then swapped points from play while McVeigh denied Colm O'Neill a goal at the expense of a '45, which was converted with aplomb by Goulding.

Down roared back with a point each from Benny Coulter and Hughes to set up a grandstand finish but Cork had sufficient experience to survive the onslaught and held on to win by a single point.

It was all hands on the deck in those final seconds and bravely Goulding intercepted a pass from Conor Maginn before being fouled by Kevin McKernan.

The final whistle brought relief for Cork and particularly for the experienced players like Canty, Murphy and Derek Kavanagh, who sustained an injury after coming on as a substitute.

Certainly it was a close call for Cork but a well-deserved victory nevertheless.

Down never once shirked the challenge and their fine performance belied their lack of big-match experience.

There was the additional disappointment for Down in that they became the first team from the county to lose in an All-Ireland decider, 50 years after the county won their first senior crown.

Cork captain, Graham Canty

2010 ALL-IRELAND
SENIOR FOOTBALL CHAMPIONSHIP FINAL

SCORERS – CORK: Daniel Goulding 0-9; Donncha O'Connor 0-5; Paul Kerrigan 0-1; Ciarán Sheehan 0-1

SCORERS – DOWN: Marty Clarke 0-3; Daniel Hughes 0-3; Paul McComiskey 0-3; Benny Coulter 0-1; Mark Poland 0-1; John Clarke 0-1; Kevin McKernan 0-1; Peter Fitzpatrick 0-1; Ronan Murtagh 0-1

CORK

Alan Quirke

Michael Shields	Eoin Cadogan	Ray Carey
Noel O'Leary	John Miskella	Paudie Kissane

Alan O'Connor   Aidan Walsh

Paul Kerrigan	Pearse O'Neill	Patrick Kelly
Daniel Goulding	Donncha O'Connor	Ciarán Sheehan

SUBSTITUTES: Nicholas Murphy for Alan O'Connor; Graham Canty *(Captain)* for Paudie Kissane; Colm O'Neill for Pearse O'Neill; Derek Kavanagh for Nicholas Murphy; John Hayes for Paul Kerrigan; Fintan Goold for Derek Kavanagh

DOWN

Brendan McVeigh

Damien Rafferty	Dan Gordon	Daniel McCartan
Conor Garvey	Declan Rooney	Kevin McKernan

Peter Fitzpatrick   Kalum King

Daniel Hughes	Mark Poland	Marty Clarke
Paul McComiskey	John Clarke	Benny Coulter *(Captain)*

SUBSTITUTES: Conor Maginn for John Clarke; Ronan Murtagh for Paul McComiskey; Brendan McArdle for Damien Rafferty; Aidan Brannigan for Kalum King; Conor Laverty for Mark Poland

CORK – 2010

Back row, left to right: (Insert: Nicholas Murphy), Graham Canty, Alan Quirke,
Paul O'Flynn, Kevin Murphy, Jamie O'Sullivan, Eoin Cotter, Colm O'Neill, Kieran O'Connor,
Noel O'Leary, Alan O'Connor, Pearse O'Neill, Fintan Goold, Ciarán Sheehan, Paul Kerrigan,
John Hayes, Conor O'Sullivan, Paddy O'Shea, Ger Spillane, Ken O'Halloran, Brian O'Regan
Front row, left to right: Seán Kiely, Daniel Goulding, Donncha O'Connor, Eoin Cadogan,
John Miskella, Michael Shields, Aidan Walsh, Paudie Kissane, Patrick Kelly, Ray Carey,
Kevin McMahon, Anthony Lynch, Derek Kavanagh

Cork manager, Conor Counihan

2010 ALL-STARS FOOTBALL SELECTION

Brendan McVeigh
(Down) 1st

Peter Kelly
(Kildare) 1st

Michael Shields
(Cork) 2nd

Charlie Harrison
(Sligo) 1st

Paudie Kissane
(Cork) 1st

Graham Canty
(Cork) 3rd

Philip Jordan
(Tyrone) 4th

Paddy Keenan
(Louth) 1st

Aidan Walsh
(Cork) 1st

Daniel Hughes
(Down) 1st

Marty Clarke
(Down) 1st

Johnny Doyle
(Kildare) 1st

Colm Cooper
(Kerry) 6th

Bernard Brogan
(Dublin) 1st

Benny Coulter
(Down) 1st

2011 ALL–IRELAND FOOTBALL FINAL

SUNDAY, SEPTEMBER 18

DUBLIN VERSUS KERRY

CROKE PARK

REFEREE: JOE McQUILLAN (CAVAN)

DUBLIN 1-12 KERRY 1-11

Memories are made of this.

September Sunday in a heaving Croke Park as Dublin goalkeeper, Stephen Cluxton, calmness personified, kicked the winning point from a high-pressure free into the Hill 16 end to beat the favourites Kerry in a pulsating All-Ireland final.

It was nothing short of sensational the manner in which Dublin won their 23rd All-Ireland title.

It was also Dublin's first victory over Kerry in an All-Ireland final since 1976.

What made the achievement all the more remarkable was the fact that Kerry had moved four points clear with seven minutes of normal time remaining following a superb point from team captain Colm Cooper.

At that juncture, very few expected any result other than a Kerry victory given their craft, experience and big match know-how.

Furthermore, Kerry had dictated the play for long stages of the second half and had outscored Dublin by 0-8 to 0-1 from the 40th minute to the 63rd.

That massive effort most likely took its toll on some of the Kerry players as they struggled with the pace of the game in the latter stages.

What happened in the closing tension-filled minutes will be discussed and debated for years to come.

Firstly, substitute Kevin McManamon latched on to a pass from Alan Brogan and brushed off the challenge of Declan O'Sullivan before striking a powerful shot to the corner of the Kerry net.

McManamon's strong, direct style caused endless problems for the Kerry defence and he once again proved his pedigree as a goalscorer.

Following McManamon's goal, Kerry appeared vulnerable and Dublin took full advantage with a point each from wing-back Kevin Nolan and Bernard Brogan.

Both points were inspirational.

Nolan was superb while Bernard Brogan made a very valuable contribution kicking six points, two from play.

His older brother Alan showed great leadership all through and scored two points from play.

He also provided the final pass for McManamon's goal.

When Kieran Donaghy scored an audacious point for Kerry to level the match in the 70th minute, a draw looked the likely outcome.

However, McManamon won the injury-time free which Cluxton converted with aplomb.

Cluxton was the calmest person in Croke Park at the final whistle and appeared oblivious to the ecstasy all around him.

There will be much soul-searching among Kerry players, management and supporters on how the Sam Maguire Cup was snatched from their grasp.

With seven minutes remaining and trailing by four points, no one realistically expected Dublin to win from that position.

It would have been impossible to comprehend that Dublin, who had only scored one point from a free in the previous 23 minutes, would outscore Kerry by 1-3 to 0-1 in the final pulsating minutes.

But that is exactly what happened on a never-to-be-forgotten day for Dublin football.

Untypically, Kerry made mistakes in the critical phase late on whereas Dublin grew in confidence following McManamon's goal.

Perhaps Kerry felt that the game was won after Cooper's score pushed them four points clear but Dublin showed tremendous character in the face of adversity.

Eoin Brosnan had a solid game for Kerry until he was substituted.

His influence was sorely missed at the heart of the Kerry defence in the frantic closing stages.

There was criticism of Dublin after their loss to Cork in the Allianz League Final earlier in the season when in a winning position.

But all that was forgotten when Cluxton's pointed free ensured a first All-Ireland for the capital since Pat O'Neill's side defeated Tyrone in the 1995 final.

Manager Pat Gilroy was the Dublin connection with the 1995 success as he came on as a substitute that day.

Make no mistake; this was a stunning victory for Dublin, not just for the manner in which Gilroy's side fashioned the comeback, but also because none of the players had ever featured in an All-Ireland final before.

Kerry had all the craft and experience with the All-Ireland medals to show for their endeavours; yet a largely inexperienced Dublin side, through sheer grit, determination and no little self-belief, produced a late comeback to rank with anything ever before witnessed on All-Ireland Football Final Sunday.

Michael Darragh Macauley, committed and hard-working throughout, was a powerhouse in the closing ten minutes as Dublin drove at Kerry with increasing menace.

Denis Bastick's work-rate was immense and he also kicked a point from play early in the second half.

Kerry struggled somewhat in the opening half and took too much out of the ball rather than adopting a more direct approach.

The Dublin backs, supported by midfielders Macauley and Bastick, along with forwards Paul Flynn, Barry Cahill, Bryan Cullen and Alan Brogan, adhered rigidly to the defensive game-plan.

Several Kerry attacks ran aground when faced with a massed defence.

Still, Cooper scored a superb goal in the 19th minute after collecting a pass from the pacey Darran O'Sullivan, which edged Kerry two points ahead.

Far from dropping their heads, Dublin remained composed and scored four points over the next 13 minutes and also succeeded in holding Kerry scoreless during that period.

Furthermore, Alan Brogan had a golden chance of a goal in the 25th minute when he took a pass from Barry Cahill, but his close-range shot was brilliantly saved by Kerry goalkeeper Brendan Kealy, who was outstanding throughout.

Conversely, the Kerry forwards were unable to make any real impact against a crowded and tight-marking Dublin defence.

Such was his concern at Dublin's dominance that Kerry manager Jack O'Connor introduced Paul Galvin in place of corner forward Kieran O'Leary as early as the 24th minute.

O'Connor obviously felt Dublin were winning more of the breaking ball and banked on Galvin to reverse the trend.

Galvin kicked a neat point just before half-time.

Still, Dublin held a one point lead at the interval, 0-6 to 1-2 and extended that advantage early in the second half through points from Bernard Brogan and Bastick.

It was then that Kerry's more experienced players responded to the challenge, most notably Darran O'Sullivan, Cooper, Donaghy and Bryan Sheehan.

Moreover, the high-fielding Anthony Maher, Sheehan's midfield partner, won good possession and used it intelligently.

The hard-working Donnchadh Walsh expended huge energy until replaced by Barry John Keane in the 51st minute.

Donaghy had a major influence on the game and might have caused even more damage had Kerry played in high ball more regularly.

The Austin Stacks clubman had a glorious chance of a goal in the 43rd minute, but opted instead to take a point.

Donaghy also made an impact during his spell at wing forward but was most effective at full-forward.

As the second half progressed, Dublin struggled to gain sufficient primary possession in the middle third as Kerry lifted the pace appreciably and played more direct football, which reaped dividends.

Kerry also channelled players back to the midfield area and won an abundance of breaking ball as a result.

As the pressure mounted, Dublin lost their shape and conceded needless frees, which were converted by the impressive Sheehan and Cooper.

Kerry also began to win possession from Cluxton's kick-outs, but Dublin continued to battle hard and never took a backward step.

Still, it looked a hopeless case for Dublin until the strong-running McManamon scored the goal that set in motion a chain of events that culminated in a dramatic pointed free for Cluxton, which secured a most famous and spectacular victory.

Dublin captain, Bryan Cullen

SCORERS – DUBLIN: Bernard Brogan 0-6; Kevin McManamon 1-0;
Alan Brogan 0-2; Stephen Cluxton 0-2; Kevin Nolan 0-1;
Denis Bastick 0-1

SCORERS – KERRY: Colm Cooper 1-3; Bryan Sheehan 0-4; Kieran Donaghy 0-2;
Paul Galvin 0-1; Declan O'Sullivan 0-1

DUBLIN
Stephen Cluxton

Cian O'Sullivan	Rory O'Carroll	Michael Fitzsimons
James McCarthy	Ger Brennan	Kevin Nolan

Denis Bastick   Michael Darragh Macauley

Paul Flynn	Barry Cahill	Bryan Cullen *(Captain)*
Alan Brogan	Diarmuid Connolly	Bernard Brogan

SUBSTITUTES: Philly McMahon for James McCarthy;
Kevin McManamon for Paul Flynn; Eoghan O'Gara for Barry Cahill;
Eamon Fennell for Denis Bastick

KERRY
Brendan Kealy

Marc Ó Sé	Tom O'Sullivan	Killian Young
Tomás Ó Se	Aidan O'Mahony	Eoin Brosnan

Anthony Maher   Bryan Sheehan

Donnchadh Walsh	Darran O'Sullivan	Kieran Donaghy
Colm Cooper *(Captain)*	Declan O'Sullivan	Kieran O'Leary

SUBSTITUTES: Paul Galvin for Kieran O'Leary; Barry John Keane for Donnchadh Walsh;
Daniel Bohan for Eoin Brosnan

DUBLIN – 2011

Back row, left to right: Paul Conlon, Eoghan O'Gara, Diarmuid Connolly, Paul Casey, James McCarthy, Ross McConnell, Michael Darragh Macauley, Barry Cahill, Michael Fitzsimons, Bernard Brogan, Cian O'Sullivan, Eamon Fennell, Denis Bastick, Declan Lally, Paul Brogan, Micheál McCarthy, Philly McMahon
Front row, left to right: Craig Dias, Ger Brennan, Rory O'Carroll, Kevin Nolan, Bryan Cullen, Stephen Cluxton, Paul Flynn, Alan Brogan, David Henry, Tomás Quinn, Dean Kelly, Kevin McManamon, Seán Murray, Ross O'Carroll, Michael Savage

Dublin manager, Pat Gilroy

2011 ALL-STARS FOOTBALL SELECTION

Stephen Cluxton
(Dublin) 4th

Marc Ó Sé
(Kerry) 3rd

Neil McGee
(Donegal) 1st

Mick Foley
(Kildare) 1st

Kevin Cassidy
(Donegal) 2nd

Karl Lacey
(Donegal) 3rd

Kevin Nolan
(Dublin) 1st

Bryan Sheehan
(Kerry) 1st

Michael Darragh Macauley
(Dublin) 1st

Darran O'Sullivan
(Kerry) 1st

Alan Brogan
(Dublin) 3rd

Paul Flynn
(Dublin) 1st

Colm Cooper
(Kerry) 7th

Andy Moran
(Mayo) 1st

Bernard Brogan
(Dublin) 2nd

2012
ALL–IRELAND
FOOTBALL FINAL

SUNDAY, SEPTEMBER 23

DONEGAL VERSUS MAYO

CROKE PARK

REFEREE: MAURICE DEEGAN
(LAOIS)

DONEGAL 2-11 MAYO 0-13

Since their narrow loss to Dublin in the 2011 All-Ireland semi-final, Donegal had been spoken of as a team that had the potential to claim ultimate honours.

And few could argue that Jim McGuinness and his dedicated and committed group of players came of age in Championship 2012.

As it transpired, Donegal were deservedly crowned All-Ireland champions following their four points victory over Mayo, in the first Ulster-Connacht final since 1948 when Cavan, captained by John Joe O'Reilly, defeated Mayo.

Donegal were strongly criticised in some quarters, much of it unwarranted, over their ultra-defensive style during the 2011 season with much negative emphasis placed on their low-scoring defeat by Dublin.

Donegal grew in confidence during the 2011 Championship campaign and that self-belief garnered by the players was put to good use as they retained their provincial crown and overcame Kerry and Cork en-route to an All-Ireland final victory over the Connacht Champions.

It was no more than a work in progress for Donegal in 2011 but through meticulous preparation, diligence and perseverance, McGuinness and his right-hand-man Rory Gallagher provided the strategy, good judgement and leadership for the players to make the quantum leap in Championship 2012.

There was unconfined joy at the final whistle in Croke Park when Donegal were crowned All-Ireland champions for just the second time in their history.

Anthony Molloy raised the Sam Maguire Cup in September 1992 when Donegal defeated Dublin in the All-Ireland final; 20 years later Michael Murphy, who along with Colm McFadden scored 1-4 in the final, had the honour of lifting the most coveted Cup in Gaelic football.

And to crown it all, Murphy sang a verse of the popular song, 'Jimmy's Winning Matches' from the steps of the Hogan Stand.

It was a day of days for McGuinness and his Donegal players, along with his backroom team and their deliriously happy supporters, who enthusiastically celebrated a famous victory.

It was evident, even during the Allianz League campaign, that Donegal's style of play had evolved, with much more emphasis on attacking football without neglecting the core duties of defending.

Donegal attacked with menace and yet had ample players behind the ball at all times to curb Mayo's attacking threat.

Donegal played six games in the 2011 championship and scored seven goals and 59 points while conceding only one goal and 54 points.

Donegal played one more game in the 2012 championship and finished with a scoring tally of eight goals and 98 points with a concession rate of three goals and 76 points.

The All-Ireland final was notable for the fact that Donegal started at a blistering pace as Murphy outfielded Kevin Keane from a superb Karl Lacey delivery and the team captain then struck a thunderous right-footed shot to the Mayo net past goalkeeper David Clarke as early as the third minute.

It would be wrong to be overly critical of Keane because Murphy, such is his power and skill, would probably have scored the goal no matter who was tracking him at that time.

It was the best possible start for Donegal who received a further boost in the 11th minute when McFadden scored an opportunist goal to leave his side 2-1 to 0-0 ahead.

McFadden took full advantage after Paddy McBrearty's attempted shot for a point came off the post and was fumbled by Kevin Keane.

To his credit, Keane recovered from that early baptism of fire and coped reasonably well for the remainder of the game.

The long ball into Murphy and McFadden reaped dividends and those early goals ultimately decided the contest.

Mayo had conceded just two goals – both against Down in the All-Ireland quarter-final – in their four games to the final, so the concession of two goals so early on was a massive setback.

Mayo goalkeeper David Clarke denied McFadden a second goal in the 14th minute with a superb block at a stage when Donegal were in complete control and were seriously threatening to overrun the Connacht champions.

It certainly looked bleak for Mayo at that juncture and no one could blame their loyal supporters if they were bracing themselves for another heavy All-Ireland final defeat similar to the ones against Kerry in 2004 and 2006.

But James Horan's side showed resilience in the face of adversity and came back strongly in the second quarter due to the growing influence of wing-back Lee Keegan.

Mayo's work-rate was immense as Colm Boyle, Keith Higgins, Donal Vaughan and Aidan O'Shea took the game to Donegal at every opportunity.

Kevin McLoughlin was highly effective in attack and kicked two points from play in the opening half, as well as providing the pass for substitute Richie Feeney's point from play late in the second half.

Ger Cafferkey was switched on to Murphy, as Mayo set about retrieving an almost impossible situation caused by the concession of those two early goals.

Michael Conroy and Enda Varley scored spectacular points as the pendulum swung in favour of Mayo, who outscored Donegal 0-7 to 0-3 in the closing 24 minutes of the opening half to leave just three points separating the sides at half-time.

Donegal lost their shape in the second quarter and at times gave the ball away cheaply, which was uncharacteristic.

Nevertheless, Donegal had extended their advantage to five points by the 48th minute as McFadden, Frank McGlynn from play and a Murphy long-range free gave the Ulster champions much-needed breathing space.

Mayo missed point-scoring opportunities during that period.

Anthony Thompson and McGlynn were superb in defence for Donegal while Mark McHugh won an amount of breaking ball and was as industrious as ever.

Lacey and the impressive Paddy McGrath along with Eamonn and Neil McGee all made their mark at various stages throughout the game for Donegal.

Substitutes Christy Toye and David Walsh also made noteworthy contributions for the Ulster champions.

Murphy and McFadden continued to influence the game during an absorbing second half.

Murphy, whose work-rate was immense all through, fisted a point in the closing stages while impressive midfielder Neil Gallagher finished off a superb move for Donegal's last point of the game.

Gallagher's midfield partner, Rory Kavanagh, was also influential for Donegal, particularly in the early stages and in the closing-tension-filled minutes.

Keegan and Jason Gibbons kicked superb points in the latter stages for a fiercely-determined Mayo side, who pressed forward relentlessly.

McGuinness deserves huge credit for turning Donegal's football fortunes around after just two seasons in charge.

No fewer than 13 of the players who featured on the Donegal team that lost by nine points to Armagh in Crossmaglen in a first-round qualifier in June 2010 played some part against Mayo.

Ten players, Paul Durcan, Paddy McGrath, Neil McGee, Karl Lacey, Frank McGlynn, Neil Gallagher, Rory Kavanagh, Mark McHugh, Michael Murphy and Colm McFadden started against Armagh in 2010 and Mayo in 2012.

Furthermore, David Walsh lined out in the Armagh game and came on as a substitute against Mayo; Christy Toye was introduced from the bench in both matches while Eamon McGee featured in the starting line-up against Mayo and came on as a substitute against Armagh.

Moreover, en route to the final, Donegal defeated Tyrone, Kerry and Cork, who between them won all eight All-Irelands from 2003 to 2010 – Kerry with four, Tyrone with three and Cork in 2010.

The Mayo players deserve total respect for the manner in which they recovered from the early setbacks and for their ability to match Donegal in all facets of play for long stages.

Donegal captain, Michael Murphy

2012 ALL–IRELAND
SENIOR FOOTBALL CHAMPIONSHIP FINAL

SCORERS – DONEGAL: Colm McFadden 1-4; Michael Murphy 1-4; Ryan Bradley 0-1; Neil Gallagher 0-1; Frank McGlynn 0-1

SCORERS – MAYO: Cillian O'Connor 0-5; Enda Varley 0-2; Kevin McLoughlin 0-2; Richie Feeney 0-1; Jason Gibbons 0-1; Lee Keegan 0-1; Michael Conroy 0-1

DONEGAL

Paul Durcan

Neil McGee   Eamon McGee   Paddy McGrath

Karl Lacey   Frank McGlynn   Anthony Thompson

Neil Gallagher   Rory Kavanagh

Mark McHugh   Leo McLoone   Ryan Bradley

Paddy McBrearty   Michael Murphy *(Captain)*   Colm McFadden

SUBSTITUTES: David Walsh for Ryan Bradley; Martin McElhinney for Paddy McBrearty; Christy Toye for Leo McLoone; Dermot Molloy for Martin McElhinney

MAYO

David Clarke *(Captain)*

Keith Higgins   Kevin Keane   Ger Cafferkey

Lee Keegan   Donal Vaughan   Colm Boyle

Barry Moran   Aidan O'Shea

Kevin McLoughlin   Jason Doherty   Alan Dillon

Enda Varley   Cillian O'Connor   Michael Conroy

SUBSTITUTES: Alan Freeman for Jason Doherty; Jason Gibbons for Michael Conroy; Richie Feeney for Enda Varley; Séamus O'Shea for Barry Moran

DONEGAL – 2012

Back row, left to right: Peter McGee, Peter Witherow, Adrian Hanlon, Daniel McLaughlin, Mark McHugh, Marty O'Reilly, Neil Gallagher, Paul Durcan, Gary McFadden, Rory Kavanagh, Paddy McBrearty, Eamon McGee, Ryan Bradley, Leo McLoone, Martin Boyle, Michael Boyle, Thomas McKinley, Christy Toye
Front row, left to right: Kevin Rafferty, Barry Dunnion, Stephen Griffin, Martin McElhinney, Anthony Thompson, Karl Lacey, Paddy McGrath, Michael Murphy, Neil McGee, Colm McFadden, Frank McGlynn, Dermot Molloy, David Walsh, Antoin McFadden, Declan Walsh

Donegal manager, Jim McGuinness

2012 ALL-STARS FOOTBALL SELECTION

Paul Durcan
(Donegal) 1st

Neil McGee
(Donegal) 2nd

Ger Cafferkey
(Mayo) 1st

Keith Higgins
(Mayo) 1st

Lee Keegan
(Mayo) 1st

Karl Lacey
(Donegal) 4th

Frank McGlynn
(Donegal) 1st

Neil Gallagher
(Donegal) 1st

Aidan Walsh
(Cork) 2nd

Paul Flynn
(Dublin) 2nd

Alan Dillon
(Mayo) 2nd

Mark McHugh
(Donegal) 1st

Colm O'Neill
(Cork) 1st

Michael Murphy
(Donegal) 1st

Colm McFadden
(Donegal) 1st

2013
ALL–IRELAND
FOOTBALL FINAL

SUNDAY, SEPTEMBER 22

DUBLIN VERSUS MAYO

CROKE PARK

REFEREE: JOE McQUILLAN
(CAVAN)

DUBLIN 2-12 MAYO 1-14

Dublin claimed their 24th All-Ireland senior football title with victory over Mayo in what was one of the most physically demanding football showpieces in living memory.

Quite frankly, it was never going to be anything less than a brutally hard and intense contest.

And that is what transpired on a boiling-hot September Sunday in Croke Park.

All-Ireland finals are about winning and Dublin did just about enough to prevail by a single point.

It was tense in the closing stages as Dublin held on to win their second All-Ireland title in three years.

Dublin forward Paul Flynn described the final as 'the hardest game I have played in my whole life'.

Dublin had used their five substitutes by the 53rd minute and left on a struggling Rory O'Carroll, later diagnosed with concussion, and Eoghan O'Gara, hampered with a hamstring injury, in the closing stages as Mayo came storming back to reduce the deficit to just one point.

That Dublin came through such a high-pressure game, under hugely stressful circumstances, underlined the quality and steel in their side.

Trailing by two points, Mayo were awarded a 20 metre free deep into injury-time but Cillian O'Connor tapped the ball over the bar.

The referee Joe McQuillan then blew the final whistle following Stephen Cluxton's kick out.

O'Connor and some other Mayo players protested afterwards that McQuillan had indicated there would be a further 30 seconds of play after the free was taken.

That, according to Mayo manager, James Horan, was why O'Connor did not attempt a goal effort.

So Dublin got over the line and, in the process, completed the Allianz League and Championship double for the county for the first time since 1976 – a remarkable achievement for Jim Gavin in his first year in charge.

There was a sense in advance of the final that this was going to be a shoot-out between the two best attacking forces in the game.

Some pundits even suggested that another game to rival the high-scoring semi-final between Kerry and Dublin was what was needed to save Gaelic football from all its perceived ills.

But a repeat of that game was highly unlikely.

That semi-final was wonderful to watch, some breathtaking football was played, but both defences leaked three goals each.

It was exhibition-like but the game is not all about high-scoring.

The art of good defending is equal to any of the other attributes of the game.

There was a marked absence of free-flowing football in the final itself, which was more notable for its intensity and physicality than the carefree football of the Dublin/Kerry semi-final.

Mayo captain Andy Moran kicked the opening point of the final but Dublin forward Diarmuid Connolly levelled matters in the fifth minute.

Dublin appeared to be a little nervous and edgy in the opening exchanges as Lee Keegan, Keith Higgins and Cillian O'Connor rowed in with a point each for Mayo.

O'Connor, who recovered from a dislocated shoulder, sustained in the semi-final against Tyrone, missed two early frees, but grew in confidence thereafter and finished with a tally of eight points.

Mayo's high-tempo game caused serious problems for Dublin in the opening fifteen minutes but the Connacht champions failed to capitalise on the scoring opportunities that came their way.

Ultimately, Mayo's first half wastefulness was to prove extremely costly.

Dublin's ability to score goals at critical stages served them well en-route to the final and Bernard Brogan flicked the ball to the Mayo net against the run of play in the 16th minute.

Mayo responded in style with points from Séamus O'Shea, O'Connor and a second one from play by impressive wing-back, Keegan, who scored in all six games during the Championship.

Dublin improved in the second quarter and began to create openings.

Mayo goalkeeper Robert Hennelly denied Ciarán Kilkenny a goal in the 24th minute but Brogan snapped up the rebound and kicked a point from play.

Michael Darragh Macauley also had a goal chance for Dublin, only for Hennelly to bring off another fine save.

Moran kicked his second point from play in the 26th minute to leave Mayo 0-8 to 1-2 ahead and in a reasonably strong position.

But the Connacht champions failed to score for the remainder of the half, during which Dublin recorded points from a Stephen Cluxton '45 and one from play by Eoghan O'Gara, who had replaced the injured Paul Mannion in the 16th minute.

Mayo's lead of a single point, 0-8 to 1-4, at half-time did not accurately reflect their dominance up to that stage, and Dublin took full advantage when midfielder Cian O'Sullivan kicked the equalising point from play shortly after the re-start.

O'Sullivan had an outstanding game for Dublin all through and was surely a contender for man of the match along with teammates, Cluxton and Brogan as well as Mayo's Keegan, Higgins, Colm Boyle and Hennelly.

Higgins, who made a significant impact in attack in the opening half, was switched to corner-back after the re-start in place of the injured Tom Cunniffe.

His presence was sorely missed in the Mayo attack in the second half.

Dublin created another goal opportunity in the 38th minute when O'Gara latched on to the ball inside the Mayo cover but his shot was deflected over the crossbar by Hennelly.

Paddy Andrews, Flynn and Brogan tacked on a point each from play in reply to a solitary Mayo free from O'Connor to push Dublin 1-9 to 0-9 ahead.

But Mayo were soon back on level terms.

Michael Conroy, who had replaced Alan Freeman, played in Moran and with Cluxton off his line the Mayo captain sent a low shot to the net in the 50th minute.

Moran displayed great leadership qualities throughout the game and finished with a tally of 1-2 from play.

Moreover, Moran's goal was Mayo's only score from play in the second half.

Dublin's fifth substitute, Denis Bastick, replaced the injured Jonny Cooper in the 53rd minute and he made a solid contribution along with the previous four replacements - O'Gara, Darren Daly, Dean Rock and Kevin McManamon.

Bastick, who came into the midfield area with O'Sullivan switching to defence, fisted a pass across the goal for Brogan to palm to the Mayo net in the 54th minute.

Brogan then brought his tally to 2-3 with a point from a free as O'Gara battled manfully with a hamstring injury.

With O'Carroll and O'Gara struggling, Dublin found it difficult to keep their composure, although Ger Brennan kicked a wonder point from play while Cluxton converted a free from a position similar to where he scored the winning point against Kerry in the 2011 final.

As Dublin's foul count increased, Cillian O'Connor kept Mayo in touch with some well-taken frees.

However, instead of attempting a goal effort, O'Connor converted a close-in free deep into injury time to cut the deficit to one point.

The referee blew the final whistle shortly after Cluxton's kick-out.

O'Connor protested that the referee had indicated there would be at least 30 seconds of play after his free was taken.

There was some consolation for Mayo supporters when their minors won the All-Ireland title with victory over Tyrone by 2-13 to 1-13 to deliver the Tom Markham Cup to the county for the first time since 1985.

Dublin played some breathtaking high-tempo football during the 2013 championship and, despite the rather ragged nature of their display in the closing stages of the final itself, Jim Gavin's side can look back on a season to remember, which yielded victories over Westmeath, Kildare, Meath, Cork, Kerry and Mayo.

Dublin had six games in the 2013 championship and scored 13 goals and 99 points while conceding five goals and 71 points.

Dublin captain, Stephen Cluxton

SCORERS – DUBLIN: Bernard Brogan 2-3; Stephen Cluxton 0-2; Eoghan O'Gara 0-2; Paddy Andrews 0-1; Diarmuid Connolly 0-1; Paul Flynn 0-1; Ger Brennan 0-1; Cian O'Sullivan 0-1

SCORERS – MAYO: Cillian O'Connor 0-8; Andy Moran 1-2; Lee Keegan 0-2; Keith Higgins 0-1; Séamus O'Shea 0-1

DUBLIN

Stephen Cluxton *(Captain)*

Philly McMahon	Rory O'Carroll	Jonny Cooper
James McCarthy	Ger Brennan	Jack McCaffrey
Michael Darragh Macauley		Cian O'Sullivan
Paul Flynn	Paddy Andrews	Diarmuid Connolly
Paul Mannion	Ciarán Kilkenny	Bernard Brogan

SUBSTITUTES: Eoghan O'Gara for Paul Mannion; Darren Daly for Jack McCaffrey; Dean Rock for Ciarán Kilkenny; Kevin McManamon for Paddy Andrews; Denis Bastick for Jonny Cooper

MAYO

Robert Hennelly

Tom Cunniffe	Ger Cafferkey	Chris Barrett
Lee Keegan	Donal Vaughan	Colm Boyle
Aidan O'Shea		Séamus O'Shea
Kevin McLoughlin	Keith Higgins	Alan Dillon
Cillian O'Connor	Alan Freeman	Andy Moran *(Captain)*

SUBSTITUTES: Michael Conroy for Alan Freeman; Cathal Carolan for Tom Cunniffe; Enda Varley for Alan Dillon; Barry Moran for Séamus O'Shea; Jason Doherty for Andy Moran

DUBLIN - 2013

Back row, left to right: Shane Carthy, Shane Supple, Kevin Nolan, Dean Rock, Paul Mannion, James McCarthy, Nicky Devereux, Michael Darragh Macauley, Paddy Andrews (in distance); Ciarán Kilkenny, Bernard Brogan, Alan Brogan, Kevin O'Brien, Declan O'Mahony, Michael Fitzsimons, Paul Flynn
Front row, left to right: Cian O'Sullivan, Ger Brennan, Diarmuid Connolly, Stephen Cluxton, Philly McMahon, Jonny Cooper, Darren Daly, Rory O'Carroll, Jack McCaffrey, Bryan Cullen

Dublin manager, Jim Gavin

2013 ALL-STARS FOOTBALL SELECTION

Stephen Cluxton
(Dublin) 5th

Colin Walshe
(Monaghan) 1st

Rory O'Carroll
(Dublin) 1st

Keith Higgins
(Mayo) 2nd

Lee Keegan
(Mayo) 2nd

Cian O'Sullivan
(Dublin) 1st

Colm Boyle
(Mayo) 1st

Michael Darragh Macauley
(Dublin) 2nd

Aidan O'Shea
(Mayo) 1st

Paul Flynn
(Dublin) 3rd

Colm Cooper
(Kerry) 8th

Seán Cavanagh
(Tyrone) 5th

James O'Donoghue
(Kerry) 1st

Bernard Brogan
(Dublin) 3rd

Conor McManus
(Monaghan) 1st

2014
ALL-IRELAND
FOOTBALL FINAL

SUNDAY, SEPTEMBER 21

KERRY VERSUS DONEGAL

CROKE PARK

REFEREE: EDDIE KINSELLA
(LAOIS)

KERRY 2-9 DONEGAL 0-12

This was as far removed from a classic final as one could get, but full credit to Kerry for coming through a torrid test to win their 37th All-Ireland title - their first in five years.

Donegal were simply unable to come close to what was a stunning performance against favourites Dublin in the semi-final when the Ulster champions scored 3-14 and conceded 17 points.

The game was ultimately decided by a mistake, as Donegal goalkeeper Paul Durcan's kick out in the 52nd minute was intercepted by the ever-alert Kieran Donaghy who showed great composure to score the game-changing goal and push Kerry four points clear.

It was cruel luck on Durcan, who was quite magnificent throughout the championship, most notably against Dublin, when he denied Diarmuid Connolly a goal in the semi-final with a top-notch save that helped turn the game decisively in Donegal's favour.

In the final itself, despite the concession of two goals, Donegal almost forced a draw in injury-time.

Michael Murphy and Paddy McBrearty combined in the build-up.

McBrearty's shot for goal was parried by Kerry goalkeeper, Brian Kelly, only for Colm McFadden to palm the rebound off the butt of the upright.

It was that close.

Kerry's first goal arrived inside the opening minute when Paul Geaney gathered a long ball from Stephen O'Brien ahead of defender Paddy McGrath and the Dingle clubman finished low past Durcan for a superb goal.

This was a final noted for packed defences and fast counter-attacking play as Kerry hit 13 wides to Donegal's eight.

Even though James O' Donoghue, later crowned 'Footballer of the Year', was held scoreless, the Killarney Legion clubman played a central linking role further out the field.

Donaghy tacked on a point from play following Geaney's quick-fire goal but, incredibly, Kerry scored just twice for the remaining 31 minutes of the half.

Paul Geaney converted a free in the 13th minute while the same player blasted over the bar with a goal chance on in the 27th minute.

Michael Murphy converted three frees for Donegal in a turgid first half; Colm McFadden landed a point from a free while Odhrán MacNiallais and Karl Lacey rowed in with a point each from play, as the sides finished level at the break, Donegal 0-6 - Kerry 1-3.

Donegal forward Darach O'Connor almost goaled in the 25th minute, but his shot took a touch off Kerry keeper, Brian Kelly and was eventually put over the end-line by Peter Crowley.

It was a clear '45 but none was given.

Michael Murphy, well marshalled by Aidan O' Mahony, nudged Donegal ahead for the first and only time in the match with a point from play shortly after the re-start but impressive Kerry defender Paul Murphy levelled matters with a superb point.

Substitute Barry John Keane converted a free in the 51st minute - only the third score at that stage of the second half - before the game changed utterly when Donaghy capitalised on the kick-out error by Durcan to score a gift-goal.

Donegal rallied, courtesy of two points from play by substitute Paddy McBrearty and one from the impressive Neil McGee to cut the deficit to a single point.

Again Kerry responded in a decisive manner; Johnny Buckley kicked a splendid point; the lively Keane tapped over a free while Donaghy brought his tally to 1-2 with a point from play.

Substitutes Dermot Molloy and Christy Toye hit back with a point each from play for Donegal before substitute Bryan Sheehan nailed a long-range free for Kerry.

Donegal came so close to levelling the match in injury-time but McFadden's fisted effort came off the post - heartbreak for Donegal - unbridled joy for Kerry, who achieved ultimate success without the injured Colm Cooper.

Kerry scored 8 goals and 102 points in their six games in the 2014 Championship and conceded 7 goals and 76 points.

Fionn Fitzgerald and Kieran O'Leary raise the Sam Maguire Cup
(Also pictured, GAA President, Liam O'Neill)

2014 ALL-IRELAND
SENIOR FOOTBALL CHAMPIONSHIP FINAL

SCORERS – KERRY: Kieran Donaghy 1-2; Paul Geaney 1-2; Barry John Keane 0-2; Paul Murphy 0-1; Johnny Buckley 0-1; Bryan Sheehan 0-1

SCORERS – DONEGAL: Michael Murphy 0-4; Paddy McBrearty 0-2; Neil McGee 0-1; Karl Lacey 0-1; Odhran MacNiallais 0-1; Colm McFadden 0-1; Christy Toye 0-1; Dermot Molloy 0-1

KERRY

Brian Kelly

Fionn Fitzgerald *(Captain)*   Aidan O'Mahony   Marc Ó Sé

Paul Murphy   Peter Crowley   Killian Young

Anthony Maher   David Moran

Donnchadh Walsh   Stephen O'Brien   Johnny Buckley

Paul Geaney   Kieran Donaghy   James O'Donoghue

SUBSTITUTES: Michael Geaney for Stephen O'Brien; Barry John Keane for Paul Geaney; Shane Enright for Fionn Fitzgerald; Declan O'Sullivan for Donnchadh Walsh; Bryan Sheehan for David Moran; Kieran O'Leary for Kieran Donaghy; Johnny Buckley (Black Card)

DONEGAL

Paul Durcan

Neil McGee   Eamonn McGee   Paddy McGrath

Anthony Thompson   Karl Lacey   Frank McGlynn

Neil Gallagher   Rory Kavanagh

Odhrán MacNiallais   Leo McLoone   Ryan McHugh

Colm McFadden   Michael Murphy *(Captain)*   Darach O'Connor

SUBSTITUTES: Christy Toye for Darach O'Connor; Paddy McBrearty for Ryan McHugh; Martin McElhinney for Odhrán MacNiallais; David Walsh for Leo McLoone; Dermot Molloy for Rory Kavanagh

Back row, left to right: (Insert: Declan O'Sullivan), Peter Crowley, Anthony Maher, Shane Enright, Bryan Sheehan, Marc Ó Sé, Kieran Donaghy, David Moran, Johnny Buckley, Brendan Kealy, Donnchadh Walsh, Killian Young, Kieran O'Leary, Stephen O'Brien, Colm Cooper
Front row, left to right: Darran O'Sullivan, Alan Fitzgerald, Mark Griffin, James O'Donoghue, Paul Murphy, Aidan O'Mahony, Fionn Fitzgerald, Brian Kelly, Pa Kilkenny, Paul Geaney, Jonathan Lyne, Barry John Keane, Michael Geaney

Kerry manager, Jack O'Connor

2014 ALL-STARS FOOTBALL SELECTION

Paul Durcan
(Donegal) 2nd

Paul Murphy
(Kerry) 1st

Neil McGee
(Donegal) 3rd

Keith Higgins
(Mayo) 3rd

James McCarthy
(Dublin) 1st

Peter Crowley
(Kerry) 1st

Colm Boyle
(Mayo) 2nd

Neil Gallagher
(Donegal) 2nd

David Moran
(Kerry) 1st

Paul Flynn
(Dublin) 4th

Michael Murphy
(Donegal) 2nd

Diarmuid Connolly
(Dublin) 1st

Cillian O' Connor
(Mayo) 1st

Kieran Donaghy
(Kerry) 3rd

James O' Donoghue
(Kerry) 2nd

2015
ALL-IRELAND
FOOTBALL FINAL

SUNDAY, SEPTEMBER 20

DUBLIN VERSUS KERRY

CROKE PARK

REFEREE: DAVID COLDRICK (MEATH)

DUBLIN 0-12 KERRY 0-9

Dublin displayed character and resilience in abundance, in dreadfully wet conditions, to chisel out a hard-fought victory over a Kerry side that came off second best in many of the personal duels, yet only lost by three points.

It was Dublin's third successive championship victory over Kerry – 2011 All-Ireland final and 2013 semi-final – in what was a titanic clash between the two counties.

Dublin's margin of victory failed to reflect their dominance in a contest that largely failed to live up to its pre-match billing.

The game was played on Dublin's terms, which was a tribute to the players and their manager Jim Gavin who proved himself to be tactically astute.

It was a highly significant victory for Dublin, given the criticism directed at the players and management following their loss to Donegal in last year's All-Ireland semi-final.

Dublin's victory was built on strong performances from their defenders; Jonny Cooper, Rory O'Carroll and Philly McMahon in the full-back line and their pacey half backs, James McCarthy, Cian O'Sullivan and Jack McCaffrey.

22-year old Brian Fenton from the Raheny club was outstanding at midfield for a Dublin side that controlled the game for long periods.

There was much talk in advance, rightly so, given their scoring tallies throughout the Championship campaign, about Dublin's much-vaunted attack.

Yet, on the biggest day of the year, it was the resolute and, at times, quite brilliant performance of the Dublin defence, as a collective unit, that proved vital to securing victory.

Kerry found it difficult to cope with Dublin's power and pace; yet the Munster Champions had a real goal chance in the 67th minute when Killian Young, set up by substitute, Kieran Donaghy, had the misfortune to let the ball slip from his grasp with just goalkeeper, Stephen Cluxton to beat.

James McCarthy collected the breaking ball and cleared to Alan Brogan - just on as a substitute for Fenton.

Brogan took the ball out of defence and played a one-two with his brother Bernard before landing a superb score to increase Dublin's lead to four points.

Kerry continued to press forward and had claims for a penalty turned down when Donaghy appeared to be fouled in a tussle for the ball.

Fenton, ably assisted by Denis Bastick and later substitute, Michael Darragh Macauley, gave Dublin an advantage at midfield against Anthony Maher and David Moran.

The Dublin defence was quite superb and restricted the Kerry starting forwards to a meagre five points from play.

Time and again, Kerry forward Colm Cooper was pulled out of his position as the Dr. Crokes clubman was forced to chase the outstanding Philly McMahon all over the pitch.

It somehow looked out of place to watch a forward of Cooper's calibre back in his own half attempting to curtail the attacking McMahon, who was on top of his game.

McMahon landed a point from play while Cooper failed to find the target – an astonishing statistic that underlines one of the reasons – and only one, why Kerry lost this final.

It was a fifth All-Ireland final loss for Cooper, who has also won four on the field of play – those victories came in 2004 and 2006 against Mayo and 2007 and 2009 against Cork.

At the post-match press conference, Kerry manager, Eamonn Fitzmaurice outlined Kerry's problems in relation to utilising Cooper's talent.

'I think it was down to Dublin having the ball and us turning over ball. If we were in possession and, if we had the ball, and were getting Colm on the ball where we wanted him to be on the ball and getting Philly McMahon defending him, we'd have been playing the game on our terms. But for a lot of the first half, we had to play the game on Dublin's terms'.

Rory O'Carroll, who had a mighty battle with Donaghy in the latter stages, was strong and assured at full-back for Dublin while James McCarthy once again displayed his class as an attacking wing-back.

Cian O'Sullivan, an injury doubt leading up to the final, was calm and confident at centre-half-back.

Jack McCaffrey, who had been ill in advance of the final, was highly effective before being replaced by John Small in the 52nd minute.

Yet, despite Dublin's impressive showing, Kerry, to their credit, persevered to the very finish and had Young capitalised on the gilt-edged opportunity late on, then it could have been all so different.

And had Donaghy won the penalty!

Close call.

Winning, losing.

It is all down to fine margins.

Kerry struggled in the forward division and were simply unable to match Dublin's intensity for the entire match.

Ultimately, Dublin fully deserved their victory – no question

Fenton hit the butt of the post with a cracking shot in the 47th minute while Paddy Andrews' blistering effort whistled narrowly wide of Brendan Kealy's post shortly after the re-start.

Goalkeeper Kealy was solid all through for Kerry.

The Kilcummin club man brilliantly saved from Dean Rock in the early exchanges to deny Dublin a goal.

Dublin deservedly held a 0-8 to 0-4 half-time advantage as Kerry struggled to make an impact.

No fewer than seven players scored for Dublin in that opening half as McMahon, McCaffrey, Fenton, Paddy Andrews and Bernard Brogan all found the range from play while Dean Rock converted two frees.

Goalkeeper and Captain Stephen Cluxton, uncharacteristically under pressure with his kick outs and in general play, sent over a free in the opening half.

In marked contrast, just two players scored for Kerry in the first half, as Paul Geaney and James O'Donoghue landed two points each from play.

O'Donoghue kicked a point from play in the second half but the Killarney Legion clubman was replaced late-on by Barry John Keane.

Geaney was also called ashore as Donaghy was introduced to the action in the 50th minute.

Donaghy caused more than a few problems for the Dublin defence but, despite his best efforts, the goal Kerry so badly needed never materialised.

Bryan Sheehan was also introduced to the fray in place of Johnny Buckley in the 44th minute in an attempt to turn the tide.

Sheehan converted a free in injury-time, which tellingly proved to be Kerry's first score for almost twenty minutes.

Darran O'Sullivan, who replaced Stephen O'Brien at half-time, made a significant impact for Kerry with two points from play.

Although Kerry manager Eamonn Fitzmaurice used his full quota of substitutes in an attempt to find a winning combination, surprisingly, Tommy Walsh was not introduced to the fray.

A Donaghy-Walsh combination in the Kerry attack could well have unlocked a Dublin defence that was certainly under-pressure in the closing stages.

Instead, Paul Galvin came in for David Moran while Paul Murphy replaced Aidan O'Mahony, who picked up a black card for a foul on Dublin substitute, Kevin McManamon.

Only defender Jonathan Lyne and O'Donoghue, from the starting line-out, scored for Kerry in the second half - a point each from play - with the other scores coming from substitutes O'Sullivan, two points from play, and Sheehan - a solitary score from a free.

Dublin captain, Stephen Cluxton

SCORERS – DUBLIN: Bernard Brogan 0-2; Dean Rock 0-2; Paul Flynn 0-2;
Brian Fenton 0-1; Philly McMahon 0-1; Alan Brogan 0-1;
Paddy Andrews 0-1; Stephen Cluxton 0-1; Jack McCaffrey 0-1

SCORERS – KERRY: James O'Donoghue 0-3; Paul Geaney 0-2;
Darran O'Sullivan 0-2; Bryan Sheehan 0-1; Jonathan Lyne 0-1

DUBLIN

Stephen Cluxton *(Captain)*

Jonny Cooper Rory O'Carroll Philly McMahon

James McCarthy Cian O'Sullivan Jack McCaffrey

Brian Fenton Denis Bastick

Paul Flynn Diarmuid Connolly Ciarán Kilkenny

Bernard Brogan Dean Rock Paddy Andrews

SUBSTITUTES: Kevin McManamon for Dean Rock;
Michael Darragh Macauley for Denis Bastick;
Michael Fitzsimons for Jonny Cooper; John Small for Jack McCaffrey;
Darren Daly for Cian O'Sullivan; Alan Brogan for Brian Fenton

KERRY

Brendan Kealy

Fionn Fitzgerald Aidan O'Mahony Shane Enright

Jonathan Lyne Peter Crowley Killian Young

Anthony Maher David Moran *(Captain)*

Donnchadh Walsh Johnny Buckley Stephen O'Brien

Colm Cooper Paul Geaney James O'Donoghue

SUBSTITUTES: Darran O'Sullivan for Stephen O'Brien;
Bryan Sheehan for Johnny Buckley; Kieran Donaghy for Paul Geaney;
Paul Galvin for David Moran;
Paul Murphy for Aidan O'Mahony (Black Card);
Barry John Keane for James O'Donoghue

Back row, left to right: Brian Fenton, David Byrne (Naomh Olaf), Dean Rock, Ciarán Kilkenny, James McCarthy, John Small, Michael Darragh Macauley, Michael Fitzsimons, Paddy Andrews, Rory O'Carroll, Cian O'Sullivan, Diarmuid Connolly, Paul Flynn, Denis Bastick, Philly Ryan, Michael Savage, Tomás Brady, Bernard Brogan
Front row, left to right: Eric Lowndes, David Byrne (Ballymun Kickhams) Philly McMahon, Stephen Cluxton, Darren Daly, Emmett Ó Conghaile, Jonny Cooper, Cormac Costello, Jack McCaffrey, Alan Brogan, Kevin McManamon

Dublin manager, Jim Gavin

2015 ALL-STARS FOOTBALL SELECTION

Brendan Kealy
(Kerry) 1st

Shane Enright
(Kerry) 1st

Rory O'Carroll
(Dublin) 2nd

Philly McMahon
(Dublin) 1st

Lee Keegan
(Mayo) 3rd

Cian O'Sullivan
(Dublin) 2nd

Jack McCaffrey
(Dublin) 1st

Brian Fenton
(Dublin) 1st

Anthony Maher
(Kerry) 1st

Mattie Donnelly
(Tyrone) 1st

Ciarán Kilkenny
(Dublin) 1st

Donnchadh Walsh
(Kerry) 1st

Conor McManus
(Monaghan) 2nd

Aidan O'Shea
(Mayo) 2nd

Bernard Brogan
(Dublin) 4th

2016
ALL-IRELAND
FOOTBALL FINAL
REPLAY

SATURDAY, OCTOBER 1

DUBLIN VERSUS MAYO

CROKE PARK

REFEREE: MAURICE
DEEGAN (LAOIS)

DUBLIN 1–15 MAYO 1–14

Dublin had to call on all their survival instincts to overcome a highly-motivated Mayo side by a single point in the replayed All-Ireland football final under lights on an early October Saturday night in Croke Park.

It was Dublin's 26th All-Ireland title and their fourth in six seasons; 2011 under the astute management of Pat Gilroy and 2013, 2015 and 2016 with Jim Gavin in charge.

Mayo conceded two own goals in the first half, scored by Kevin McLoughlin and Colm Boyle, in the 2016 drawn encounter before coming back to force a replay through a superb point from Cillian O'Connor deep into injury-time.

Mayo manager Stephen Rochford opted to bring in goalkeeper Robert Hennelly for the replay 13 days later in place of David Clarke, but the change backfired.

Hennelly failed to hold on to a ball in the 40th minute and was then forced to haul down Paddy Andrews to concede a penalty.

The Breaffy clubman picked up a black card for that foul and was replaced by Clarke, whose first task was to pick the ball out of the net after Diarmuid Connolly converted the penalty.

Clearly, the Mayo management felt that Hennelly was the better goalkeeper to deliver a match-winning kick-out strategy but that is not how it transpired on a day when the game was decided by the smallest of margins.

Dublin manager Jim Gavin made three changes from the drawn encounter; Michael Fitzsimons, Paddy Andrews and Paul Mannion were drafted into the starting line-up in place of David Byrne, Michael Darragh Macauley and Bernard Brogan.

The impressive Dean Rock scored 8 points – two from play - in the opening half – to help Dublin establish a 0-10 to 1-6 advantage at the break.

Dublin's other scores in a hard, physical and combative first half came from Kevin McManamon and Diarmuid Connolly.

Rock kicked two scores from play and converted a free in the early exchanges as Dublin moved four points clear just after the six minute mark.

McManamon also landed a point from play during that dominant phase for the Leinster champions.

Mayo soon found their rhythm and had levelled the match by the 13th minute through a point apiece from open play by Paddy Durcan and Andy Moran along with two frees from Cillian O'Connor.

Dublin defender John Small was fortunate not to pick up a black card for a hand trip on Andy Moran in the 8th minute before O'Connor converted the resultant free.

Mayo lifted the intensity no end from the time Durcan nailed their first score in the 7th minute and were rewarded with a stunning goal from Lee Keegan, set up by Aidan O'Shea, in the 18th minute.

That goal edged Mayo ahead for the first time.

Significantly, Keegan picked up a black card for a foul on Connolly in first half injury-time after Hennelly's kick out was intercepted.

Clearly the dismissal of Keegan represented a massive setback for Mayo and his presence was sorely missed, particularly in the closing quarter, when the game was in the balance.

Connolly had kicked a wonder point from play under pressure shortly before Keegan's dismissal.

By that stage, Dublin had also lost one of their star defenders, Jonny Cooper, who had been issued with a black card in the 20th minute.

Cooper was replaced by David Byrne, left out of the starting line out in favour of Michael Fitzsimons, who justified his selection with a 'Man of the Match' performance.

Like in the drawn encounter, Mayo started the second half in sprightly fashion with a point each, on this occasion, from brothers Cillian and Diarmuid O'Connor.

Rock levelled the game for the fifth time with his ninth point of the match, before Hennelly's mistake cost Mayo dearly.

Hennelly dropped a Paul Flynn effort before dragging down the alert Andrews as he gathered the loose ball.

Connolly's aim from the penalty was true and, as it transpired, Dublin never relinquished the lead thereafter.

The pace never dropped; Cillian O'Connor and Kevin McLoughlin rowed in with a point each for Mayo; substitute Bernard Brogan, played in by Macauley, landed a point in response for Dublin, before Durcan replied with a spectacular second point from play.

But Dublin's ace in the pack was young substitute Cormac Costello, who kicked three magnificent points from play, under pressure, to demonstrate his class as a player of the highest quality.

Macauley, too, was highly effective off the bench and his trademark runs gave Dublin a distinct advantage and put the Mayo defence under pressure.

Cillian O'Connor converted three frees in the course of a frantic closing ten minutes but the Mayo captain missed a last-gasp free kick from a difficult position in the 76th minute when his shot into the Hill 16 end drifted narrowly wide at the near post.

In the extraordinarily tension-filled closing minutes, the highly-impressive Fitzsimons had the chance to score an insurance point, but instead opted to pass to Bernard Brogan, whose kick was blocked down.

The game was played at a ferocious intensity right from the throw-in and both teams displayed unbelievable character and commitment.

So Dublin prevailed by a single point to become the first county since Kerry in 2006 and 2007 to achieve the two-in-row.

It was also the first time, since the double winning teams of 1976 and 1977, that Dublin won back-to-back All-Ireland titles.

The 2016 drawn final will be remembered for Mayo's two own goals in the opening half and Cillian O'Connor's magnificent levelling point from play deep into injury-time while the replay, once again, underlined Dublin's character to grind out a result in the face of extreme pressure.

SCORERS – DUBLIN: Dean Rock 0-9; Diarmuid Connolly 1-1; Cormac Costello 0-3; Bernard Brogan 0-1; Kevin McManamon 0-1

SCORERS – MAYO: Cillian O'Connor 0-9 ; Lee Keegan 1-0; Paddy Durcan 0-2; Kevin McLoughlin 0-1; Andy Moran 0-1; Diarmuid O'Connor 0-1

DUBLIN

Stephen Cluxton *(Captain)*

| Philly McMahon | Jonny Cooper | Michael Fitzsimons |
| James McCarthy | Cian O'Sullivan | John Small |

Brian Fenton   Paul Flynn

| Diarmuid Connolly | Kevin McManamon | Ciarán Kilkenny |
| Paul Mannion | Dean Rock | Paddy Andrews |

SUBSTITUTES: David Byrne for Jonny Cooper (Black Card);
Bernard Brogan for Paddy Andrews;
Michael Darragh Macauley for Paul Mannion;
Cormac Costello for Kevin McManamon;
Eric Lowndes for John Small; Darren Daly for Cian O'Sullivan

MAYO

Robert Hennelly

| Brendan Harrison | Donal Vaughan | Keith Higgins |
| Lee Keegan | Colm Boyle | Paddy Durcan |

Séamus O'Shea   Tom Parsons

| Kevin McLoughlin | Aidan O'Shea | Diarmuid O'Connor |
| Jason Doherty | Andy Moran | Cillian O'Connor *(Captain)* |

SUBSTITUTES: Stephen Coen for Lee Keegan (Black Card);
Conor O'Shea for Donal Vaughan;
David Clarke for Robert Hennelly (Black Card)
Barry Moran for Andy Moran; Alan Dillon for Jason Doherty;
Chris Barrett for Colm Boyle

Back row, left to right: Michael Darragh Macauley, David Byrne, Brian Fenton, Shane Carthy,
Dean Rock, James McCarthy, Ciarán Kilkenny, Robbie McDaid, Eoghan O'Gara,
John Small, Paddy Andrews, Shane Clayton, Bernard Brogan,
Tomás Brady, Denis Bastick, Eric Lowndes, Paul Flynn, Michael Savage
Front row, left to right: Con O'Callaghan, Cormac Costello, Colm Basquel, Stephen Cluxton,
Philly McMahon, Darren Daly, Cian O'Sullivan, Diarmuid Connolly, Jonny Cooper,
Paul Mannion, Michael Fitzsimons, Kevin McManamon

Dublin manager, Jim Gavin

2016 ALL-STARS FOOTBALL SELECTION

David Clarke
(Mayo) 1st

Brendan Harrison
(Mayo) 1st

Jonny Cooper
(Dublin) 1st

Philly McMahon
(Dublin) 2nd

Lee Keegan
(Mayo) 4th

Colm Boyle
(Mayo) 3rd

Ryan McHugh
(Donegal) 1st

Brian Fenton
(Dublin) 2nd

Mattie Donnelly
(Tyrone) 2nd

Peter Harte
(Tyrone) 1st

Diarmuid Connolly
(Dublin) 2nd

Ciarán Kilkenny
(Dublin) 2nd

Dean Rock
(Dublin) 1st

Michael Quinlivan
(Tipperary) 1st

Paul Geaney
(Kerry) 1st

2017
ALL–IRELAND
FOOTBALL FINAL

SUNDAY, SEPTEMBER 17

DUBLIN VERSUS MAYO

CROKE PARK

REFEREE: JOE McQUILLAN
(CAVAN)

DUBLIN 1–17 MAYO 1–16

Dublin completed the much talked about three-in-a-row – the first team from the capital since 1923 to achieve that notable distinction, with a one-point victory over a Mayo side that never once took a backward step in their relentless pursuit of victory but, heartbreakingly, came up short once again.

Dublin defeated Mayo by a single point in the 2013 final and then overcame the same opposition by the same slender margin in the 2016 decider, following a replay.

And when referee Joe McQuillan called time on the 2017 All-Ireland Final, it was Dublin who had again prevailed, courtesy of a pointed free in injury-time from the impressive Dean Rock.

Stephen Cluxton grabbed the headlines again when he became the first player in the history of the game to lift the Sam Maguire Cup on four occasions.

This was a quite remarkable and unique achievement and testament to Cluxton's leadership and innate goalkeeping skills.

Young Dublin forward, Con O'Callaghan scored a superb goal to set Hill 16 alight and rock Mayo after just 83 seconds to underline his class as one of the rising stars of the game.

O'Callaghan, from the Cuala club, showed maturity way beyond his years, to take on the vastly-experienced Colm Boyle before finishing impressively past All-Star goalkeeper, David Clarke.

As it transpired, it was the only goal Dublin scored in the game, as Mayo battened down the hatches thereafter with a high-quality defensive display.

Dublin suffered a setback when Jack McCaffrey was forced to retire with a knee injury in the 9th minute and his defensive skills and electrifying pace were sorely missed.

Mayo recovered from the concession of the early goal and seriously challenged Dublin for the remainder of the opening half.

Six Mayo players scored from play in the first half alone, including the in-form Andy Moran, who landed three points.

Jason Doherty, too, showed impressive form and scored two points with one each coming from Donal Vaughan, Kevin McLoughlin, Cillian O'Connor and Colm Boyle, which helped Mayo establish a 0-9 to 1-5 advantage at the break.

Despite O'Callaghan's early goal, Dublin struggled to get to their usual tempo in the first half; Dean Rock scored three points – 2 from frees - while John Small and Eoghan O'Gara, who started in place of Niall Scully, tacked on a point each from play.

Aidan O'Shea and Tom Parsons controlled midfield in the opening half, as Mayo won no fewer than six of Cluxton's kick outs.

The tide turned in Dublin's favour in the second half when Cluxton opted for the short kick out strategy which he executed to near perfection.

Both goalkeepers were called upon early in the second half; firstly Cluxton brought off a top-class save to deny Jason Doherty a goal while, moments later, David Clarke rescued Mayo with a fine block from a Paul Mannion shot.

Lee Keegan considerably restricted the influence of Ciarán Kilkenny and, moreover, the 2016 'Footballer of the Year' scored a stunning goal in the 54th minute after taking a pass from Andy Moran.

Keegan's goal, at such a critical stage, could have proved decisive against lesser opposition, but this Dublin team are clearly a cut above the rest.

Dublin have earned an impressive reputation as a team that possesses the mobility, skill and the hard edge necessary to eke out victories in close tense games and that steel and resilience was evident again in the All-Ireland final.

John Small was issued with a second yellow card for a foul on Mayo defender Colm Boyle in the 47th minute but before Cillian O'Connor could take what was an eminently scorable free, Vaughan rushed over and struck the Dublin defender.

Consequently, both teams were reduced to 14 players – but Mayo suffered most, as the referee threw the ball in and the chance of another score was lost.

And so, in a nail-biting finish, Dublin again prevailed, despite the fact that Mayo held a two-point advantage with 7 minutes of normal time remaining.

Mayo were in a strong position at that juncture but, instead, it was Dublin who responded to the challenge with points from Paul Mannion, James McCarthy and Dean Rock.

McCarthy was magnificent throughout, particularly so in the second half, when the Ballymun Kickhams clubman kicked two points from play.

McCarthy's strong running from midfield also caused problems for the Mayo defence.

Still, Mayo refused to wilt and Cillian O'Connor kicked a superb point to level the match for the 11th time in the 68th minute.

There was cruel luck for Mayo in the 71st minute as Cillian O'Connor hit the far upright with a free kick – from a similar distance to the one the team captain drove wide in the 2016 replayed final.

And, ultimately, it all came down to almost the final kick of the game in the 76th minute, from which the ice-cool Dean Rock duly delivered the match-winning score after substitute, Diarmuid Connolly was fouled.

Lee Keegan threw a GPS tracker in Rock's direction as he was about to strike the last free, but it failed to distract the Ballymun Kickhams sharpshooter.

There was more controversy in the closing seconds also as Ciarán Kilkenny picked up a black card for a foul on Keegan.

So then, sheer delight for Dublin and yet more heartbreak for brave Mayo – another case of what might have been for a group of players that have shed blood, sweat and tears for the cause.

Importantly, and not for the first time, Dublin kept their composure, under intense pressure, to grab another famous victory, thus becoming the first county since Kerry, 1984-1986, to claim the coveted three-in-a-row.

Mayo, who played ten games in the 2017 Championship, have now lost in 9 All-Ireland senior finals and drawn two since their last success back in 1951; those defeats came in 1989, 1996 (draw and replay), 1997, 2004, 2006, 2012, 2013, 2016 (draw and replay) and 2017.

Enough to break the spirit of a whole county never mind a football team.

2017 ALL–IRELAND
SENIOR FOOTBALL CHAMPIONSHIP FINAL

SCORERS – DUBLIN: Dean Rock 0-7; Paul Mannion 0-3; Con O'Callaghan 1-0; James McCarthy 0-2; Eoghan O'Gara 0-1; John Small 0-1; Diarmuid Connolly 0-1; Brian Fenton 0-1; Kevin McManamon 0-1

SCORERS – MAYO: Cillian O'Connor 0-7 ; Andy Moran 0-3; Lee Keegan 1-0; Kevin McLoughlin 0-2; Jason Doherty 0-2; Donal Vaughan 0-1; Colm Boyle 0-1

DUBLIN

Stephen Cluxton *(Captain)*

| Jonny Cooper | Philly McMahon | Michael Fitzsimons |
| John Small | Cian O'Sullivan | Jack McCaffrey |

Brian Fenton   James McCarthy

| Ciarán Kilkenny | Dean Rock | Con O'Callaghan |
| Paul Mannion | Eoghan O'Gara | Paddy Andrews |

SUBSTITUTES: Paul Flynn for Jack McCaffrey; Diarmuid Connolly for Paddy Andrews; Kevin McManamon for Eoghan O'Gara; Bernard Brogan for Paul Flynn; Niall Scully for Con O'Callaghan; Cormac Costello for Paul Mannion; Ciarán Kilkenny (Black Card)

MAYO

David Clarke

| Chris Barrett | Brendan Harrison | Paddy Durcan |
| Lee Keegan | Colm Boyle | Keith Higgins |

Séamus O'Shea   Tom Parsons

| Kevin McLoughlin | Aidan O'Shea | Donal Vaughan |
| Jason Doherty | Cillian O'Connor *(Captain)* | Andy Moran |

SUBSTITUTES: Diarmuid O'Connor for Séamus O'Shea; Stephen Coen for Colm Boyle; Conor Loftus for Andy Moran; David Drake for Jason Doherty; Danny Kirby for Kevin McLoughlin; Ger Cafferkey for Keith Higgins

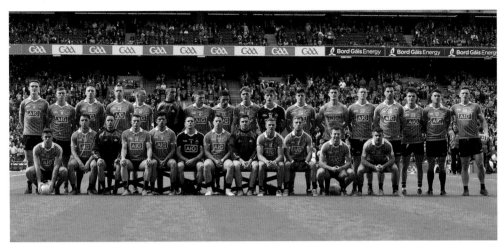

Back row, left to right: Brian Fenton, Con O'Callaghan, Eoghan O'Gara, Dean Rock,
Ciarán Kilkenny, James McCarthy, John Small, Niall Scully, Michael Fitzsimons,
Evan Comerford, Brian Howard, Diarmuid Connolly, Denis Bastick, Michael Darragh Macauley,
Eric Lowndes, Bernard Brogan, Paul Flynn
Front row, left to right: David Byrne, Cormac Costello, Shane Carthy, Darren Daly,
Cian O'Sullivan, Stephen Cluxton, Philly McMahon, Paddy Andrews, Paul Mannion,
Jonny Cooper, Jack McCaffrey, Kevin McManamon

Dublin manager, Jim Gavin

2017 ALL-STARS FOOTBALL SELECTION

David Clarke
(Mayo) 2nd

Chris Barrett
(Mayo) 1st

Michael Fitzsimons
(Dublin) 1st

Keith Higgins
(Mayo) 4th

Colm Boyle
(Mayo) 4th

Cian O'Sullivan
(Dublin) 3rd

Jack McCaffrey
(Dublin) 2nd

Colm Cavanagh
(Tyrone) 1st

James McCarthy
(Dublin) 2nd

Dean Rock
(Dublin) 2nd

Aidan O'Shea
(Mayo) 3rd

Con O'Callaghan
(Dublin) 1st

Paul Mannion
(Dublin) 1st

Paul Geaney
(Kerry) 2nd

Andy Moran
(Mayo) 2nd

2018
ALL-IRELAND
FOOTBALL FINAL

SUNDAY, SEPTEMBER 2

DUBLIN VERSUS TYRONE

CROKE PARK

REFEREE: CONOR LANE
(CORK)

DUBLIN 2-17 TYRONE 1-14

Dublin footballers claimed the much sought after four-in-a-row with a six-point victory over a strong-willed and competitive Tyrone team that gave it everything on All-Ireland Final Sunday, but ultimately came up short against a quite exceptional side.

Thus Dublin completed the four-in-a-row joining the Kerry teams of 1929-1932 and 1978-1981 along with the Wexford 1915 to 1918 sides – one hundred years previously.

Stephen Cluxton raised the Sam Maguire Cup for the fifth time since 2011 when Bryan Cullen was captain and Pat Gilroy was manager.

It was Dublin's 28th All-Ireland title and their sixth in 8 seasons – five of those under the management of Jim Gavin.

This is an ultra-golden phase for Dublin who had to endure a barren period between 1996 and 2010 when no All-Irelands were annexed.

Impressive Dublin came through unbeaten in Championship 2018 with wins over Wicklow, Longford, Laois, Donegal, Tyrone, Roscommon and Galway in the All-Ireland semi-final.

The final was Dublin's eighth game whereas Tyrone played 10 games in total, including the final.

Tyrone lost to Monaghan in the Ulster quarter-final and to Dublin in the All-Ireland quarter-final phase 2 clash in Omagh.

Tyrone had victories over Meath, Carlow, Cavan, Cork, Roscommon and Donegal before overcoming Monaghan in the All-Ireland semi-final.

In the final itself, despite a less than assured start, as a confident Tyrone side raced 0-5 to 0-1 ahead after 16 minutes, Dublin recovered in style to fashion yet another famous victory.

Tyrone clearly held the upperhand in the early exchanges but once Paul Mannion converted a penalty, the game changed decisively in favour of Dublin.

The referee adjudged that Tiernan McCann fouled Mannion and the Kilmacud Crokes clubman dispatched the penalty beyond Niall Morgan with aplomb.

Strangely, that goal had a demoralising effect on Tyrone as Dublin swept clear with breathtaking pace, power and scoring touch.

Con O'Callaghan sidestepped Michael McKernan to superbly play in Niall Scully for Dublin's second goal to put serious pressure on Tyrone, who battled manfully but paid a heavy price for poor marksmanship.

Dublin outscored Tyrone by 2-6 to 0-1 in a blistering second quarter to move seven points clear – 2-7 to 0-6 - at half-time.

Dublin defender Cian O'Sullivan had to retire injured in the 27th minute and was replaced by the experienced Michael Fitzsimons, who performed admirably in the heat of battle.

Dublin struggled defensively in the opening quarter but Tyrone missed too many scoring opportunities during their stretch of dominance to substantially benefit from their impetus.

In fact, Tyrone shot 16 wides in the course of the match to Dublin's six – a statistic that underlines the major difference between the teams.

Far too often, Tyrone took shots from outside the scoring zone whereas Dublin were much more potent on the scoring front.

In fact, Dublin shot no wides in the second half which illustrated their composure in front of the posts.

Tyrone undermined a vast amount of hard graft with poor decision making and shot selection whereas Dublin's patience on the ball was rewarded with scores.

Still, a spirited Tyrone side reduced the margin to just four points in the closing stages as Dublin finished the game with 14 players after John Small picked up a second yellow in injury-time.

However, Tyrone missed scoring chances at that critical juncture that could have narrowed the margin still further until Dublin displayed the mental resolve necessary to close out the game.

Tyrone's Kieran McGeary was black carded in the 49th minute and was replaced by Harry Loughran.

Colm Cavanagh, the only Tyrone player to have previously played in an All-Ireland final, proved effective when switched to full-forward in the latter stages of the game and was fouled by Philly McMahon for a penalty in the 67th minute.

Peter Harte clinically drove the penalty past Cluxton and that was quickly followed by a pointed free from Tyrone substitute Lee Brennan to reduce the deficit to four points.

Again, Dublin responded and finished impressively with some neat points, including the final score of the match from substitute, Michael Darragh Macauley.

Dublin forward Brian Howard superbly fielded a high ball in injury-time to relieve pressure as Tyrone came in search of a second goal.

Tyrone outscored Dublin by 1-8 to 0-10 in the second half to illustrate their perseverance and resilience against a team at the peak of their powers.

Jack McCaffrey, who had to retire with a cruciate knee ligament injury in the 2017 All-Ireland Final, produced a 'Man of the Match' display through his darting runs and clever defending.

McCaffrey also scored a point from play.

Ciarán Kilkenny was highly influential and landed three points from play to underline his class as an exceptional player.

Interestingly, Kilkenny had never previously scored in an All-Ireland senior final, so the 2018 decider was especially significant for the proud Castleknock clubman.

Dublin defender Eoin Murchan was superb in his first All-Ireland final while Brian Fenton, who has never lost a match in inter-county championship football, once again delivered a strong display and kicked two points from play at a crucial stage in the second half.

There was so much conversation in 2018 about the Super 8's which provided the opportunity for the best teams to emerge at the All-Ireland quarter-final stage.

The four teams to come through the qualifiers were Monaghan, Tyrone, Kildare and Roscommon and they were joined by the provincial champions, Donegal, Kerry, Dublin and Galway.

Monaghan and Galway emerged from Group One while Dublin and Tyrone came through from Group 2.

Dublin defeated Galway in the All-Ireland semi-final by 1-24 to 2-12 while Tyrone had a 1-13 to 0-15 victory over Monaghan at the same stage.

Dublin scored an incredible 17 goals and 169 points in their 8 games in the 2018 Championship while conceding just six goals and 105 points.

Kerry minors completed the historic five-in-a-row with victory over Galway in the All-Ireland final by 0-21 to 1-14 in the first year that the age limit was reduced to under 17.

Dublin captain, Stephen Cluxton

SCORERS – DUBLIN: Dean Rock 0-7; Paul Mannion 1-1; Ciarán Kilkenny 0-3; Niall Scully 1-0; Brian Fenton 0-2; Brian Howard 0-1; Jack McCaffrey 0-1; Kevin McManamon 0-1; Michael Darragh Maculey 0-1

SCORERS – TYRONE: Peter Harte 1-1; Lee Brennan 0-3; Connor McAliskey 0-3; Cathal McShane 0-2; Mark Bradley 0-2; Tiernan McCann 0-1; Kieran McGeary 0-1; Pádraig Hampsey 0-1

DUBLIN

Stephen Cluxton *(Captain)*

Philly McMahon	Cian O'Sullivan	Jonny Cooper
John Small	Eoin Murchan	Jack McCaffrey

Brian Fenton   James McCarthy

Niall Scully	Con O'Callaghan	Brian Howard
Paul Mannion	Ciarán Kilkenny	Dean Rock

SUBSTITUTES: Michael Fitzsimons for Cian O'Sullivan; Cormac Costello for Niall Scully; Kevin McManamon for Paul Mannion; Darren Daly for Eoin Murchan; Eric Lowndes for Jonny Cooper; Michael Darragh Macauley for Dean Rock

TYRONE

Niall Morgan

Tiernan McCann	Ronan McNamee	Pádraig Hampsey
Michael McKernan	Mattie Donnelly *(Captain)*	Rory Brennan

Colm Cavanagh   Conor Meyler

Kieran McGeary	Niall Sludden	Cathal McShane
Mark Bradley	Peter Harte	Connor McAliskey

SUBSTITUTES: Lee Brennan for Conor Meyler; Frank Burns for Niall Sludden; Richie Donnelly for Connor McAliskey; Harry Loughran for Kieran McGeary (Black Card); Declan McClure for Cathal McShane; Ronan O'Neill for Mark Bradley

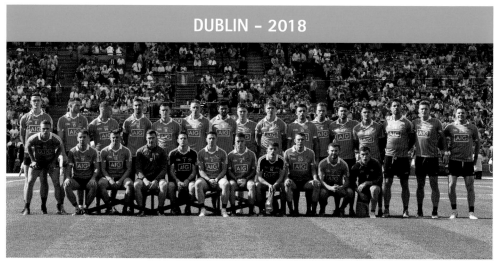

Back row, left to right: Brian Fenton, Dean Rock, Ciarán Kilkenny, James McCarthy, Con O'Callaghan, Eoghan O'Gara, Cian O'Sullivan, John Small, Michael Fitzsimons, Niall Scully, Jonny Cooper, Bernard Brogan, Eric Lowndes, Michael Darragh Macauley, Paul Flynn, Kevin McManamon
Front row, left to right: Paul Mannion, Cormac Costello, Brian Howard, Paddy Andrews, Stephen Cluxton, Philly McMahon, Eoin Murchan, Evan Comerford, Darren Daly, Jack McCaffrey, Colm Basquel

Dublin backroom team

Back row, left to right: Jim Gavin (Manager), Brian Doyle, Ray Boyne, Mick Deegan, John Courtney, Niall Barry, Chris Farrell, Tony Boylan, David Byrne, James Allen, Shane O'Hanlon, Jason Sherlock, Declan Darcy
Front Row, left to right: Bernard Dunne, David Boylan, Daniel Davey, Anne Marie Kennedy, Mick Seavers (Dublin County Board Chairman), Kieran O'Reilly, Frank Roebuck, Séamus McCormack, Kiaran O'Malley, Jimmy Gavin (Jim Gavin's father)

2018 ALL-STARS FOOTBALL SELECTION

Rory Beggan
(Monaghan) 1st

Jonny Cooper
(Dublin) 2nd

Colm Cavanagh
(Tyrone) 2nd

Pádraig Hampsey
(Tyrone) 1st

Karl O'Connell
(Monaghan) 1st

James McCarthy
(Dublin) 3rd

Jack McCaffrey
(Dublin) 3rd

Brian Fenton
(Dublin) 3rd

Brian Howard
(Dublin) 1st

Paul Mannion
(Dublin) 2nd

Ciarán Kilkenny
(Dublin) 3rd

Ryan McHugh
(Donegal) 2nd

David Clifford
(Kerry) 1st

Conor McManus
(Monaghan) 3rd

Ian Burke
(Galway) 1st

O'Callaghan then sent over a point but Kerry again responded and points from Clifford, Geaney and O'Shea reduced the deficit to the minimum by the 45th minute.

Incredibly, Dublin recorded their first wide of the game in the 44th minute when Mannion missed the target.

Brian Fenton, who has never lost a match in inter-county championship football, was superb for Dublin all through, as was James McCarthy and Jonny Cooper, who overcame the disappointment of his dismissal on a second yellow card just before half-time in the drawn game.

Kerry scored just two points in the closing 25 minutes of the replay – one apiece from O'Shea and Clifford – while Dublin pulled clear and tacked on seven points, including two each from Mannion and Rock.

Niall Scully, McCarthy and Kilkenny all found the range from play as Dublin held possession and probed at appropriate times.

Kilkenny's fourth point from play in the 46th minute came from a truly exquisite pass from substitute, Diarmuid Connolly, who replaced the injured Jack McCaffrey at half-time.

McCaffrey had been outstanding in the drawn match and scored 1-3 to emerge as the top scorer from play in a 'Man of the Match' performance.

Connolly was denied a goal late in the game through a fine save from Kerry keeper, Shane Ryan, who also blocked O'Callaghan's follow up effort at the expense of a '45, converted by Rock.

Kerry had a golden opportunity to level the match in the 52nd minute but Stephen O'Brien's goal-bound shot was saved by Cluxton.

Dublin scored 1-17 of their total from play while Dean Rock, who scored 0-10 in the drawn encounter, converted a '45 late in the game.

Kerry conceded no free within Rock's range in the replay.

Kerry will find it difficult to accept this defeat, particularly so because of missed opportunities in the drawn encounter when momentum was clearly on their side and the fact that Dublin created history in the replay – an incredible achievement - which eluded Kerry in 1982.

No one could lay any blame at the door of this young Kerry team who prepared assiduously and played with determination and skill across both the drawn match and replay.

Dublin played nine games in Championship 2019 with wins over Louth, Kildare, Meath, Cork, Roscommon and Tyrone before accounting for Mayo in the All-Ireland semi-final by 3-14 to 1-10.

Dublin then drew with Kerry in the All-Ireland final before emerging victorious in the replay by 1-18 to 0-15 to create history.

Dublin captain, Stephen Cluxton

SCORERS – DUBLIN: Paul Mannion 0-4; Ciarán Kilkenny 0-4; Con O'Callaghan 0-4; Dean Rock 0-3; Eoin Murchan 1-0; James McCarthy 0-1; Niall Scully 0-1; David Byrne 0-1

SCORERS – KERRY: Seán O'Shea 0-5; David Clifford 0-5; Paul Geaney 0-4; Adrian Spillane 0-1

DUBLIN

Stephen Cluxton *(Captain)*

Jonny Cooper	Michael Fitzsimons	David Byrne

Eoin Murchan	John Small	Jack McCaffrey

Brian Fenton   James McCarthy

Niall Scully	Ciarán Kilkenny	Brian Howard

Paul Mannion	Con O'Callaghan	Dean Rock

SUBSTITUTES: Diarmuid Connolly for Jack McCaffrey; Philly McMahon for Eoin Murchan; Cormac Costello for Niall Scully; Kevin McManamon for Paul Mannion; Cian O'Sullivan for David Byrne; Michael Darragh Macauley for Brian Howard

KERRY

Shane Ryan

Jason Foley	Tadhg Morley	Tom O'Sullivan

Brian Ó Beaglaoich	Paul Murphy *(Captain)*	Gavin Crowley

David Moran   Jack Barry

Diarmuid O'Connor	Seán O'Shea	Adrian Spillane

Paul Geaney	David Clifford	Stephen O'Brien

SUBSTITUTES: Jack Sherwood for Brian Ó Beaglaoich; Gavin White for Adrian Spillane; Tommy Walsh for Diarmuid O'Connor; Killian Spillane for Paul Murphy; James O'Donoghue for Jack Barry; Dara Moynihan for Gavin Crowley

DUBLIN – 2019 (REPLAY)

Back row, left to right: Brian Fenton, Dean Rock, Con O'Callaghan, Ciarán Kilkenny,
James McCarthy, Michael Darragh Macauley, John Small, Paul Mannion,
Michael Fitzsimons, Diarmuid Connolly, Bernard Brogan, Eric Lowndes,
Niall Scully, Evan Comerford, Kevin McManamon
Front row, left to right: David Byrne, Cormac Costello, Brian Howard, Cian O'Sullivan,
Stephen Cluxton, Philly McMahon, Eoin Murchan, Paddy Small,
Paddy Andrews, Jack McCaffrey, Jonny Cooper

Dublin manager, Jim Gavin

2019 ALL-STARS FOOTBALL SELECTION

Stephen Cluxton
(Dublin) 6th

Michael Fitzsimons
(Dublin) 2nd

Ronan McNamee
(Tyrone) 1st

Tom O'Sullivan
(Kerry) 1st

Paddy Durcan
(Mayo) 1st

Brian Howard
(Dublin) 2nd

Jack McCaffrey
(Dublin) 4th

Brian Fenton
(Dublin) 4th

David Moran
(Kerry) 2nd

Paul Mannion
(Dublin) 3rd

Seán O'Shea
(Kerry) 1st

Michael Murphy
(Donegal) 3rd

David Clifford
(Kerry) 2nd

Cathal McShane
(Tyrone) 1st

Con O'Callaghan
(Dublin) 2nd